MW01068927

Aldersgate and Athens

Aldersgate and Athens

*John Wesley and the Foundations
of Christian Belief*

WILLIAM J. ABRAHAM

BAYLOR UNIVERSITY PRESS

© 2010 by Baylor University Press
Waco, Texas 76798

Cover Design: Amy Stirnkorb
Cover Image: The Revd. John Wesley. A.M. Founder of the Methodist Society, LC-USZ62-5824, courtesy of the Library of Congress

Library of Congress Cataloging-in-Publication Data

Abraham, William J. (William James), 1947-
  Aldersgate and Athens : John Wesley and the founda-
tions of Christian belief / William J. Abraham.
      p. cm.
  "The material that follows represents the substance of a series of
lectures delivered at Barker Road Methodist Church in Singapore"--Pref.
  Includes bibliographical references and index.
  ISBN 978-1-60258-246-0 (pbk. : alk. paper)
  1. Wesley, John, 1703-1791. 2. Conversion--Christianity--
Case studies. 3. God--Knowableness. 4. Faith. I. Title.
  BX8495.W5A66 2009
  287.092--dc22
                                    2009027661

Printed in the United States of America on acid-free paper.

To Alvin Plantinga,

Provocative Pioneer

Table of Contents

Preface

The material that follows represents the substance of a series of lectures delivered at Barker Road Methodist Church in Singapore. I am grateful to the Reverend Malcolm Tan for his kind invitation to deliver these lectures and for the wonderful hospitality I enjoyed during my stay in Singapore. They attempt to show that John Wesley, in his day, offered important insights into the epistemology of theology that can readily bear fruit in our own time. I hope that they may encourage others to explore the full range of insights into the epistemology of theology scattered throughout his works. The material has been slightly revised since its delivery, but I have not sought to eliminate the original form.

Chapter 1

Faith and the Promises of God

> In the evening I went very unwillingly to a society in Aldersgate-Street, where one was reading Luther's preface to the Epistle to the Romans. About a quarter before nine, while he was describing the change which God works in the heart through faith in Christ, I felt my heart was strangely warmed. I felt I did trust in Christ, Christ alone for salvation: And an assurance was given me, that he had taken away *my* sins, even mine, and saved *me* from the law of sin and death.[1]

For many Methodists, the experience of John Wesley captured in these famous words remains a fascinating event worthy of celebration and extended reflection. They even have a name for it: the Aldersgate experience. The name is taken from Aldersgate Street in London where on May 24, 1738, Wesley had the heartwarming experience that launched him into his career as one of the truly great evangelists of the church in the West. A short time before Aldersgate, Wesley had come back from Georgia: a failure in love, a failure in his vocation, and a failure in his spiritual life. After Aldersgate he became a transformed man. Despite efforts by recent scholars of Wesley to dislodge it, Aldersgate remains a powerful symbol for the significance of John Wesley. Even outside of Methodism, Aldersgate is sufficiently recognized to be taken as a symbol of the pivotal place of conversion in early Methodism; there is a lot of merit to this reading.[2] However, we have not begun to fathom the intellectual resources opened up by Wesley through his own carefully calibrated account of Aldersgate. In this book, I wish to explore these intellectual resources in some detail.

In a moment I shall allow Wesley to supply his own interpretation of what happened. It is, however, worth asking at the outset: why does Aldersgate continue to gain our attention? There are two obvious reasons: first, the story itself is fascinating. Here is a stuffy Englishman—an Anglican priest, an Oxford don, an incurable workaholic, and a failed missionary—who has a life-changing experience of God that was to become the foundation of a Christian movement that then became a spiritual home for millions of people across the world.[3] There are so many sides to the story that repetition fails to dampen the enthusiasm for hearing it all over again. I remember when, as a preteen, I first heard it from Reverend Twinem of the Ballinamallard Methodist church when I was being prepared for full church membership. I had nothing in my family or personal history to prepare me for the encounter with Wesley. Frankly, it scared me spiritually. On the one hand, I was attracted by the drama of the story; on the other, I was repelled by the possible spiritual consequences to be had if I were to take it seriously. I was glad that we moved house and church that year so that I did not have to deal with it at that point in my life. Nevertheless, after all the intervening years, I still read the narrative with great interest.

The second reason why the Aldersgate story is fascinating is the intrinsic attraction of its central feature: the focus on certainty and assurance. Whatever we say about what happened on that fateful evening, one thing is clear: Wesley went into it full of fears, uncertainty, and doubts; he came out the other end with certainty and confidence. We know that he wobbled on occasion even immediately after Aldersgate. Richard P. Heitzenrater's brilliant analysis has sorted out why this was the case.[4] He has shown that Wesley was in reality trying out the theology of the Christian life taught to him by the Moravians. It took him some time to sort through what was essential and what was secondary. It is important, however, to keep our focus. Wesley found an assurance at Aldersgate that really did revolutionize his life and ministry.

Whatever his shortcomings, John Wesley had full possession of his intellectual faculties. After Aldersgate, he was confident about God; he was sure and certain about God; he had found forgiveness and pardon from God; he had come to know God. We might say he had come to filial, as opposed to propositional, philosophical or speculative knowledge of God. He now knew that he was a child of God and that he was really loved by God. This knowledge was not a matter of intellectual skill; it did not come from his philosophical or theological training at Oxford; it did not depend on his ability to grasp and understand arguments or propositional evidence. This knowledge was intimate, internal and filial knowledge of God.

The intellectual challenge posed by Wesley's experience at Aldersgate is as deep today as it was in the eighteenth century. The issue can be expressed very simply: how can Wesley claim to be so sure of God? How can he claim to have knowledge of God? Most theologians and philosophers find it astonishing to claim to have knowledge of God. If they allow any claims at all about God, then they are much more modest about the options. We may hope that God exists; we may believe that God exists; we may accept that God exists;

we may confess that God exists; we may have faith that God exists; we may choose to hold that God exists; we might even allow that it is plausible or probable that God exists. To say without qualification that God exists, or that we are certain that God exists, is wholly illegitimate. This is a shocking claim to advance in serious intellectual circles whether they are modern or postmodern. For modernists the problem is that belief in God is not a true, justified belief; for postmodernists the worry is that all our beliefs are relative to context, social location, gender, and the like, so that claims to knowledge are really disguised expressions of power.

Three other factors add to the shock. First, consider the content of Wesley's claim. He claims to know that the Triune God exists. The God that Wesley claims to know is not the God of deism, mere theism, or general revelation. The God Wesley claims certainty about is the God of special revelation, of Scripture, of the Creeds, of the classical, ecumenical tradition. Wesley's proposal is over the top; it underwrites a rich, robust theism.

Second, the claim to know this God, the Triune God of the church, does not depend on natural theology, that is, on the classical arguments for the existence of God.[5] Wesley was well aware of the standard arguments. As far as he was concerned, they were rickety and unstable. When he tried them on for intellectual size, he found himself ready to commit suicide. He invites us to check out their cogency and then gives his own assessment.

> But in a point of so unspeakable importance do not depend on the word of another; but retire for a while from the busy world, and make the experiment yourself. Try whether your reason will give you a clear, satisfactory evidence of the invisible world. After the prejudices of education are laid aside, produce your strong reasons for the existence of this. Set them all in array; silence

all objections, and put all your doubts to flight. Alas, you cannot, with all your understanding. You may perhaps repress them for a season. But how quickly will they rally again, and attack you with redoubled violence! And what can poor reason do for your deliverance? The more vehemently you struggle, the more deeply you are entangled in the toils. And you find no way to escape.[6]

As with so much of what Wesley said, this stark claim was modified on other occasions, as when he allowed that the "heathen" do have some knowledge of God by inference.[7] As it stands, however, in this instance Wesley clearly eschewed the help of any appeal to classical natural theology.

Third, Wesley held to the possibility of knowledge of God, fully aware of the radical mystery of God and of his presence in Christ; he was equally aware of the vast tracks of moral and natural evil that surround us. Thus he was not running away from the classical problems that have been a puzzle, if not a nightmare, for both students of theology and ordinary believers.[8] He had a keen sense of the mystery enshrined in the Trinitarian and christological faith of the church. He also had a keen sense of the problem of evil. Hence Wesley's claim to filial knowledge of God was made in the face of the critical intellectual worries that have dogged the Christian faith since its inception.

In this book I wish to investigate why it was that Wesley was so confident and bold in his assertions. Beyond that I wish to explore whether or not Wesley's writings have anything of value to offer the contemporary pilgrim. I aver that Wesley does indeed have something important to say to us regarding the relationship between faith and reason. We need, however, careful unpacking of the precise arguments that Wesley developed rather than general, abstract, global gestures.[9] I wish to suggest that in and around Aldersgate, Wesley hit upon three very interesting sources providing evidence for the truth of the Christian faith. If we read the *Journal* entries carefully, we can see that Wesley's narrative provides a seamless interweave of these three themes. These sources of evidence, I shall argue, carry real weight both singly and combined. In one of the three cases I think that Wesley was extremely astute in unpacking the evidence available to us. He takes up the other two themes, albeit haphazardly, in various places. He was aware of the possibilities and drew on them informally and tacitly, effectively milking them evangelistically. My aim will be to make explicit the arguments that lie below the surface of Wesley's intellectual journey.

The three sources of evidence at hand can be identified more formally in this fashion. First, there is the evidence drawn from the fulfillment of divine promises; second, there is the evidence taken from personal awareness of divine forgiveness and pardon; and third, there is the evidence of the power of God in our lives. In dealing with this network of evidence I have an agenda with two components. First, I shall try to unpack the logic that is at stake in each of these arguments. Second, I wish to bring Wesley's various proposals into conversation with more recent work in the epistemology of theology. In short I shall seek to retrieve and restate Wesleyan insights that are available to us today.

So let us get to work on the first leg of the argument, the argument from the fulfillment of divine promises at Aldersgate. Wesley begins his account of Wednesday, May 24, 1738 in this fashion: "I think it was about five this morning, that I opened my Testament on those words . . . 'There are given unto us exceeding great and precious promises, even that ye should be partakers of the divine nature' (2 Peter 1:4)."[10] On Sunday, June 4 he writes, "Was indeed a feast-day. From the time of my rising till past one in the afternoon, I was praying, reading the Scriptures, singing praise, or calling sinners to repentance. All these days I scarce remember to have opened the New Testament, *but upon some great and precious promise. And I saw more than ever, that the Gospel is in truth but one great promise, from the beginning to the end.*"[11] What was the promise that Wesley had discovered between May 24 and June 4? From the context I think the promise was something like this: Those who give up the quest for God on the basis of their own righteousness or merit and trust entirely in God's work in Christ will come to experience a sense of pardon for all past sins. Laying hold on this promise as articulated by his Moravian friend and temporary spiritual mentor, Peter Böhler, Wesley renounced all dependence on his own works of righteousness and, using all the means of grace at his disposal, he sought in prayer "for this very thing, justifying, saving faith, a full reliance on the blood of Christ shed for *me*; a trust in Him, as *my* Christ, as my sole justification, sanctification, and redemption."[12] Then, as he put it in his famous words about Aldersgate, he gained the faith he had sought in response to the gospel promise.

> In the evening I went very unwillingly to a society in Aldersgate-Street, where one was reading Luther's preface to the Epistle to the Romans. About a quarter before nine, while he was describing the change which God works in the heart through faith in Christ, I felt my heart was strangely warmed. I felt I did trust in Christ, Christ alone for salvation: And an assurance was given me, that he had taken away *my* sins, even mine, and saved *me* from the law of sin and death.[13]

The temptation at this point is to jump immediately to the issue of assurance and from there move to the matter of the witness of the Holy Spirit and make that the focus of our attention. To make that move would be moving much too quickly. As Wesley rightly noted in the June entry, there is in fact something extremely interesting happening here, namely, the fulfillment of the promise of the gospel. My contention is this: the fulfillment of the promise was in part the source of Wesley's assurance. In his experience at Aldersgate, God's promise—the one great promise of the gospel—had been partially fulfilled in his own life. This fulfillment provided Wesley with evidence of the truth of the gospel.

How does this evidence work? How should we think of its force? The argument is inductive and experiential in spirit and informal in structure. Wesley, with many others, had come to experience for himself the fulfillment of a significant divine promise. It is this fact that is the focus of the argument. We might express the issue more formally in this way: If many people have satisfied to a significant extent the conditions laid down for a sense of pardon from the guilt and power of sin, and if they, or a large proportion of them, then receive such a sense of pardon and power, this provides us with evidence for the truth of the claim that this promise was indeed made by a being with the wherewithal and the will to make good on that promise.[14] Wesley puts the argument with exemplary succinctness into two sentences: "What the Scripture promises, I enjoy. Come and see what Christianity has done here; and acknowledge it is of God."[15] This is the fundamental logic of the argument. It is a matter of acknowledging God's action in fulfillment of promises.

Wesley's Aldersgate experience stands at this point as a paradigm of a host of cases that might be cited as instances of fulfillment of divine promises. If all we had was Wesley's experience, then the argument would be weak. Wesley's experience, however, by no means stands alone. Early Methodist autobiographical and biographical literature is full of this kind of testimony. Moreover, it can be found well outside the bounds of Methodism across the whole Christian spectrum. Thus the positive evidence for the extent of the fulfillment of the promise of the gospel is very significant indeed.

It is worth pausing and asking if the evidence of Wesley's own experience can count for much *in his own case*. In fact Wesley had already felt the force of the evidence culled from Scripture, the Moravians, Peter Böhler and the other witnesses brought to Wesley by Böhler. It was precisely this that shook him to the core of his being. So we must not discount the evidence available to Wesley *before* his own personal experience. Yet we also have to allow some weight to Wesley in his own particular case. Given the testimonies available to him and his background beliefs, I think that the evidence for Wesley must count as significantly strong. It is this strength that surely shows up in his conviction that the gospel is in truth but one great promise. It is very hard to see Wesley deploying this understanding of the gospel before Aldersgate. Thus it is important to register his own clear avowals about the difference in allegiance and conviction that Aldersgate precipitated.

It is also worth noting that Wesley quite explicitly insists (in keeping with the impression that Böhler and others made on him) that the evidence is not just for the person who has experienced the fulfillment of divine promise, but also even for those who have not. He lays this argument out more formally in the following passage:

> Perhaps you will say, "But this internal evidence of Christianity affects only those in whom the promise is fulfilled. It is no evidence to me." There is truth in this objection. It does affect them chiefly, but it does not affect them only. It cannot, in the nature of things, be so strong an evidence to others as it is to them. And yet it may bring a degree of evidence, it may reflect some light on you also.
>
> For, First, you see the beauty and loveliness of Christianity, when it is rightly understood; and you are sure there is nothing to be desired in comparison of it.

Secondly. You know the Scripture promises this, and says, it is attained by faith, and by no other way.

Thirdly. You see clearly how desirable Christian faith is, even on account of its own intrinsic value.

Fourthly. You are a witness, that the holiness and happiness above described can be attained no other way. The more you have laboured after virtue and happiness, the more convinced you are of this. Thus far then you need not lean upon other men; thus far you have personal experience.

Fifthly. What reasonable assurance can you have of things whereof you have not personal experience? Suppose the question were, Can the blind be restored to sight? This you have not yourself experienced. How then will you know that such a thing ever was? Can there be an easier or surer way than to talk with one or some number of men who were blind, but are now restored to sight? They cannot be deceived as to the fact in question; the nature of the thing leaves no room for this. And if they are honest men, (which you may learn from other circumstances,) they will not deceive you. Now, transfer this to the case before us: And those who were blind, but now see,—those who were sick many years, but now are healed,—those who were miserable, but now are happy,—will afford you also a very strong evidence of the truth of Christianity; as strong as can be in the nature of things, till you experience it in your own soul: And this, though it be allowed they are but plain men, and, in general, of weak understanding; nay, though some of them should be mistaken in other points, and hold opinions which cannot be defended.[16]

While Wesley misleadingly calls the evidence "internal evidence," this is surely a fine articulation of the argument for the fulfillment of divine promise.

Before I take up some objections to the line of argument I am developing it is important to note the kind of argument we have on offer here: a) The claim is a modest one. It provides some evidence for the truth of the gospel; it does not provide any kind of deductive proof or conclusive evidence. b) The evidence is contextual. We are not here engaging in offering universal reasons available to everybody; we are speaking of evidence that is person-relative, that is, available to those who have sought God as Wesley did. c) The evidence is *prima facie* evidence; that is, it can be defeated in various ways. Indeed it took Wesley time to process what was going on and to reach a settled judgment about the truth of the gospel for himself. d) The evidence is not subject to quantitative calculation or explicitly formal analysis; it is constituted by rational considerations that rightly persuade the intellect but that do so as a matter of judgment. e) The evidence generally works with other evidence, even though it adds its own weight to the total evidence available. Thus it is best seen as working within a network of evidence that persuades the believer of the truth of the gospel; it is part of an informal, cumulative case argument.

Let us now consider a network of objections that can readily be made against this whole line of thinking. I shall lay out two sets of related objections and see where they take us. The objections are both philosophical and theological in nature. I shall articulate them in terms of questions that will naturally occur to the thoughtful reader. Beyond that I wish to consider a potentially stronger version of the argument from the fulfillment of divine promises.

First, does not this whole way of thinking presuppose that Christianity is first and foremost an explanatory system subject to endless debate, rather than a moral and spiritual response to divine initiative as presented in the gospel? Surely (it will be said) you have turned the Christian faith into a grand intellectual theory rather than a practical matter of radical faith and obedience to God? Worse still, have you not turned God into an object alongside other objects whose primary role is to provide an explanation for a certain kind of religious experience? Second, surely (it will be said) God is not some kind of agent among other agents? Surely God is the ground of all agency and being, rather than one being among other beings dragged in to explain this or that worldly event? To put the matter bluntly, you have corrupted pure religion by making it a theoretical rather than a practical affair; and you have turned God into an intellectual idol that has to fit into an explanatory scheme.

Here is my reply. On the second count I plead guilty. I am indeed construing God as a divine agent who acts in the world. Indeed this is exactly the vision of God that makes the most sense of Wesley's experience of God. With the whole Christian tradition Wesley saw God not as some abstract deity best captured in terms of, say, being, or ground of being, process, or even agency, but as an intimate personal agent who is identified precisely in terms of action predicates. Thus God is the one who created the world, redeemed it through the work of his Son, sent the promised Holy Spirit, has forgiven us our sins and the like. To reject the idea of God as an agent is simply to unravel the critical conception of God at the heart of the Christian gospel. This is not to say that God is simply one more agent alongside other natural, or human, or even angelic agents. God's agency transcends all other agency precisely because God is the creator and sustainer of all other agents, both visible and invisible. The best way to state this, however, is not to reach for abstract nouns like indeterminate agency, being, process, ground of being, or the like. The very idea of God's transcendent agency is best captured in terms of a vision of creation and providence that relies precisely on the transcendent actions of God. Hence this objection has no purchase against Wesley or the extension of Wesley's vision that I am pursuing here.

God is best understood as an agent, especially so, if, as Wesley suggests, the gospel is best understood as in truth one great promise from the beginning to the end. We might say (with apologies to Anselm) that God is the greatest conceivable promise-giver and promise-keeper. God is that promise-giver and promise-keeper than which none greater can be thought. And to make minimal sense of that notion we need to think of God as an agent.

As to the first objection (that I have turned the faith into a grand explanatory theory), I concede immediately that the objection has hold of a pivotal insight. Christianity is not first and foremost a theory or network of explanations. To stick to Wesley's terms, Christianity is one great promise that brings us to God and recreates in us the image of God. As we see from the heart of Wesley's overall theological vision as developed in his canonical sermons, the Christian faith can be seen soteriologically, that is, as a proposal directed to the moral and spiritual healing of our lives.[17] Moreover, a person can respond to the gospel promise without giving a second thought to the kind of theoretical consideration that I have developed from Wesley. When we are confronted with the depths of our sin and with the extraordinary promise of salvation, our first thought is not intellectual but practical. As we see in Wesley, his concern was focused on how he had come to experience what God had promised. Thus he had to give up all attempts at earning the favor of God, and he set about waiting upon God in all the means of grace at his disposal. His concerns were eminently practical and spiritual. Thus far the objection carries a profound insight into the fundamental character of the Christian faith.[18]

However, it is simply a mistake to think that this insight excludes a secondary and legitimate analysis that explores the cognitive and intellectual material that is buried within these practical and spiritual concerns. As we have seen, Wesley himself is not at all opposed to articulating the argument from divine promises. He was very well aware of this side of the Christian faith; he was at times passionately committed to exploring how best to articulate the cognitive side of critical aspects of the Christian faith. Hence Wesley rejected the setting up of an oppositional dichotomy between the practical and the theoretical, between the spiritual and the explanatory. While the Christian faith is thoroughly practical and spiritual, it is also theoretical and explanatory. Hence taking the practical seriously does not preclude the proper exploration of the tacit intellectual moves that lie below the practical and the spiritual.

Moreover, once we put the practical and theoretical into proper perspective, it is entirely possible for the ordinary believer to experience the fulfillment of the promises of God without having in hand some theoretical account of the intellectual resources that are at his or her disposal. Thus in no way are we making the spiritual dependent on the theoretical. The spiritual has its own integrity. When we move to the theoretical, we are not undermining the practical and the spiritual; we are simply seeing a further dimension to our lives that deserves to be unpacked and explored. If you like, we are making the implicit explicit; we are coming to terms with the underlying intellectual significance of what God has done in our lives in the fulfillment of divine promises. Such work has its own payoff; it can strengthen commitment to God by bringing its own measure of assurance and illumination to the believer.

Insisting on the legitimacy of the explanatory and theoretical is, of course, a risk. Once we stake a theoretical claim, it is open to theoretical objections. This takes me to a second set of worries. I grant your theoretical rights at this point (it will be said), but surely your argument is inappropriate and weak. Explanatory arguments must be more stringent than the kind that you propose here. Surely at this point we need apt scientific inquiry where we have objective investigation with proper control groups, so that we can test if the divine promise proposed by Wesley really is fulfilled. We need careful study so that we can make sure that the relevant conditions are met and the relevant outcomes are secured. Even if we can get past this worry, surely the evidence in Wesley's own *Journal* shows how weak the evidence really is. He wobbles all over the place in his spiritual life, so that the sense of pardon and power that he identified on May 24 is actually an insignificant episode in his spiritual journey that has been grossly exaggerated in the hagiography that so besets the pious, Methodist reception of Wesley.[19] Hence in reality the argument from the fulfillment of divine promise is so weak that Wesley would have been wise to say nothing about it. Therefore your effort to unpack and enrich his position is a lost cause.

Everything hinges here on how we read the logic of the argument. The core of the objection is that proper explanation must fit the pattern that is central to scientific explanation. In this analysis all causal explanations ultimately must be expressed in terms of the logic of prior conditions and predicted outcomes that are characteristic of good scientific investigation. To get at the truth of such claims we need proper scientific investigation complete with neutral observers, control groups, clarity of conditions and predictions and so on.

I grant immediately that this kind of work has been central to much scientific investigation. I leave aside entirely how well this fits all scientific investigation, though I note that this claim is highly contested in much recent philosophy of science. Moreover, I am happy to allow any and all kinds of psychological investigation of Christian claims with or without control groups. Indeed I would point out that we cannot say in advance what the outcome of such research would be. In fact, I think that such investigation would likely confirm and not undermine the claims I am advancing here.

I deny, however, the core assumption at stake in this objection. The core assumption is that all explanations are scientific explanations and all putative explanations are subject to the paradigm of scientific explanation. However, no such claim is on offer in the argument developed heretofore. The explanation offered is in terms of personal explanations, that is, events and states of affairs are explained in terms of the action and agency of God, rather than in terms of impersonal causes, general laws, events and the like. However we articulate the logic of personal explanations, personal explanations remain entirely legitimate. We constantly explain events and states of affairs as brought about by the actions and agents who do what they do because of their nature, disposition, motives, reasons and the like. Thus the proper analogy to invoke is not science but everyday personal explanations readily understood by ordinary folk. The logic is not that of prior conditions and predictions but that of promise and fulfillment. The promise comes with various conditions, and the fulfillment is tied to the content of the promise. The conditions identified in this case are, of course, religious and spiritual. As we have seen, Wesley thought of it in this way: God has promised that if we give up seeking salvation by works and seek the face of God in the appointed means of grace, then we will come to experience a sense of pardon and deliverance from sin. He met the conditions and the fulfillment happened. Consequently he was entitled to take the fulfillment as evidence of the reality of God as an agent who fulfilled the promises of the gospel. This argument holds as it stands, and it is simply beside the point to say that we do not have proper scientific investigation. We are not dealing with science but with theology; and it is a category mistake to force theology into the procrustean bed of scientific explanation and argument.

What then of the other half of the argument? Is the evidence in Wesley's case too weak to count for much? Does he wobble all over the place so that in fact his own experience in the end is so subject to fluctuation and doubt that it evaporates into thin air? In fact Wesley wobbles less than we are wont to believe. He does indeed come to reassess his experience, updating it in the light of later experiences, seeking to find a more nuanced account of what happened at Aldersgate and the initial significance he assigned to it.[20] But a careful reading of the *Journal* for May and June shows that he remained remarkably consistent and stable in his sense of pardon and deliverance. However, even if we go for a severe weakening of the evidence in Wesley's case, the argument as a whole still stands. What is at stake is not simply the evidence of one individual, but the cumulative evidence scattered throughout a wealth of autobiographical and biographical literature across space and time. It is the full weight of that evidence that is at stake; such evidence remains even if we subtract what we can glean from Wesley. Even then, I think that Wesley has his own testimonial evidence to add to the wide body of evidence available elsewhere.

This leads to a final objection of a very different kind. Surely (it will be said) we can find much stronger evidence for the fulfillment of divine promises than the sort Wesley mentions here. Should we not look for a much stronger version of the argument deployed? This is especially true if we follow Wesley's remarkable insight averring that the commands of God are covered promises.[21] When God tells us to do something, the command is an implicit promise that God's agency will make possible the outcome of the command. So consider the following narrative: In the middle of the 1960s a young Christian from Southern California, after his conversion at sixteen, was attending an independent Pentecostal church in Almonte outside Los Angeles. His name was Dennis Balcombe. At the service the wife of the main American preacher suddenly started speaking in fluent Hebrew. She had never heard Hebrew spoken before. After delivering her message, another person received the interpretation in English and shared it with the congregation. An American Jew who happened to be in the church that day confirmed the accuracy of the message. The heart of the message was that he was going to be used by God as a missionary in China. In essence we have a combination of promise, prediction, and command. In time this young Christian was drafted into the First Air Cavalry, spent some time in Vietnam, and thereafter ended up in China, where he had a pivotal ministry. So much so, that in 2002 a native Chinese Christian leader (Zhang Ronglaing) referred to him as the second Hudson Taylor.[22] Here surely is a much stronger argument from the fulfillment of divine promise than the rather rickety argument gleaned from an obscure English evangelist from Oxford in the eighteenth century. So why not cut to the chase and go for the kind of conclusive evidence we actually have on hand in our own day and generation? Why not appeal to divine promises that are fulfilled in a much more robust fashion in the present?

It is important to be clear about the argument we are articulating in this chapter. Our quarry is an argument from divine promise. Our quarry is not an argument from the experience of divine speaking or from personal revelation. The example I have just given yields, interestingly, evidence on both fronts. Thus there is here a very interesting claim to special revelation accompanied in this instance by a double miracle, the miracle of speaking in a foreign language and the miracle of its translation or interpretation. The argument from the experience of special divine revelation, however, takes us into a whole other topic, so I want to ensure that we bracket it from consideration. Wesley is in fact committed to very robust views of divine revelation, but that is a topic that needs extended treatment in its own right. So with that distraction out of the way, let us proceed to the matter in hand.

What is at issue here, happily, is an aggressive, friendly amendment rather than a rejection of the motion before the house. Let us call this the Balcombe amendment. I welcome the Balcombe amendment, but I also urge caution. I welcome it because this kind of material has had a far more important role in convincing folk of the truth of the gospel than modern theologians have allowed. Such material shows up in the history of the early church in Acts, for example, and thereafter; it has an underground place in the church that has yet to be historically retrieved. We know also that from Wesley onward much of modern theology (both "liberal" and "conservative") has been vehemently and often dogmatically hostile to this kind of narrative. The effort to dismiss Wesley as an "enthusiast," as laying claim to special inspiration or personal revelation, was one that stalked him within the Anglican intellectual establishment. He was right to take up his pen and deal with it forthrightly.[23] With Wesley I welcome the openness to the kind of phenomena narrated here. I marvel at the fancy intellectual footwork, the name-calling, and the extremes of denial and ignorance that modern and contemporary theologians have resorted to in order to keep this kind of material from the attention of theological students. Tackling that issue, however, is a labor for another day and another occasion.

Coming back to the topic at hand, the obvious point to make is that nothing in what I have said precludes appeal to the Balcombe amendment. On the contrary, we can take this additional evidence on board so long as we properly unpack the logic that lies behind it. It is precisely the unpacking of the relevant logic at the base of the argument that I have sought to provide in this chapter. Once unpacked in terms of the fulfillment of divine promises, we can add the evidence from the Balcombe amendment to the evidence instantiated in Wesley's case. We are adding to our toll of evidence rather than subtracting from it or undermining what we already possess. We are enriching the body of evidence with further cases of promise-fulfillment.

So why then do I urge caution? I do so for two reasons. First, we need authentication of the kind of material represented by the Balcombe amendment. Much of our evidence for this kind of case is journalistic and anecdotal, yet it is evidence that is not to be sniffed at skeptically. Such evidence plays a crucial role in our fund of knowledge and in practices of epistemic justification.[24] This is the case both in the academy and in a host of everyday situations. It is also the case, of course, that much of the kind of evidence instantiated in the Balcombe case is readily laced with pious exaggeration and hostility toward serious investigation. In fact, it is often embedded in systems of Christian belief that on other grounds are subject to serious intellectual criticism. Hence we must unpack what is at stake, sorting the intellectual wheat from the chaff. At this point Wesley is important because he can aid in drawing us into the deep structures of the Christian tradition developed canonically in the one, holy, catholic and apostolic Church.[25] It is the truth of that wider belief system that should detain us; we must distinguish this vision of the faith from sensational or unbalanced versions of the faith. Therefore we need to work further on this kind of material and how it can be deployed as evidence for the truth of the gospel.

Second, what is especially important about Wesley's version of the argument presented here is that it is available to everyone. Specific promises of the kind presented in this alternative instantiation of the argument from the fulfillment of divine promises are relatively rare. Wesley would have considered them extraordinary. In their nature they are therefore scattered and sporadic. Moreover, one can always keep them at arms length, for they are always removed from the ordinary believer, mediated by testimony that is often from afar. The evidence from divine promises as Wesley presents it is potentially in hand. Indeed Wesley's ministry was built on the assumption that everyone should be presented with the gospel so that they may find for themselves the evidence made available from the fulfillment of the promises of God. Thus we do not have to go hunting after wonderful, but rare and spectacular, fulfillment of divine promises in faraway lands or faraway history. "There are given unto us great and precious promises, even that ye should be partakers of the divine nature (2 Peter 1:4)."[26] There is in fact that promise of promises, the promise at the heart of the gospel: those who give up on their own righteousness and seek God in the means appointed by the church will find a genuine sense of pardon and deliverance from sin. This promise lies in hand today as much as it lay in hand to Wesley. It would surely be a great mistake to neglect such a rich treasure buried in the foundations of our faith. How the dramatic kind of evidence we find in the Balcombe-type case is to be handled, what special difficulties may afflict it and how it is to be compared with the evidence from promise-fulfillment are issues we shall take up in our third chapter. As we will see, Wesley has some very interesting comments on these scores that are well worth considering.

In the meantime we would do well to heed Wesley's insight into the significance of divine promise-fulfillment. In our own journey of faith, just like Wesley, we can make the same discovery that he did: "What the Scripture promises, I enjoy. Come and see what Christianity has done here; and acknowledge it is of God."

Chapter 2

Faith and Personal Experience of God

We are exploring the relation between faith and reason with substantial help from our Father in God, John Wesley. The topic of faith and reason, of course, is a vast one that has pre-occupied both learned theologians and ordinary Christians from the very beginning of the Christian faith. The amount of material available on the relationship between faith and reason is absolutely staggering. And the debate rages on today. Indeed the last forty years have seen an amazing turnaround in the discussion. When I was trained in philosophy in the late 1960s in the splendid philosophy department at Queen's University in Belfast, I could not initially find anyone to teach me philosophy of religion. It was simply assumed that religious discourse lacked intellectual content, so there was no point in discussing the relation between faith and reason. Faith did not have any intellectual content (it might have emotional content), so there was no possibility of reasoning about it. Since the early 1970s, we have witnessed a veritable revolution in the field. This is true in theory of knowledge in general and in the epistemology of Christian theology in particular. Indeed the options have become so robust and diverse that it is difficult to keep up with the discussion. The time is long overdue to revisit the Wesleyan tradition and look at it afresh from the vantage point of developments in the discussion over the last forty years. My hope is to stimulate a conversation between Wesley and the contemporary discussion. It would be premature to claim that there is or can be a characteristic Wesleyan epistemology of theology; I think, however, that Wesley brings to our attention a raft of very significant proposals that deserve to be heard in the contemporary debate.

In the last chapter I noted that in and around the Aldersgate experience there are three different kinds of evidence visible below the surface. There is the evidence from the fulfillment of divine promises, the evidence from personal experience of God, and the evidence from the power of God. In this chapter I want to explore the second of these moves, that is, the appeal to personal experience of God. In this case Wesley provides much more than an implicit argument that needs to be made explicit; he actually seeks to unpack the underlying argument; and he does so on numerous occasions with enthusiasm. As we proceed, we shall see that in terms of the contemporary discussion there are in fact at least three ways of fleshing out his proposals. Hence we can bring the Wesleyan material right into the heart of the recent discussion. Our first task is to get hold of what Wesley has to offer in some detail.

Understanding Wesley is by no means an easy assignment, for he tackles the issue of personal experience of God from more than one angle. Thus we have to attend to what he says about faith as a source of evidence, and we have to explore what he says about the inner witness of the Holy Spirit as a source of evidence. In the first case Wesley's favorite text is Hebrews 11:1: "Now faith is the assurance of things hoped for, the conviction of things not seen."[1] In the second case Wesley's favorite text is Romans 8:15-17: "For you did not receive a spirit of slavery to fall back into fear, but you have received a spirit of adoption. When we cry, 'Abba! Father!' it is that very Spirit bearing witness with our spirit that we are children of God. . . ."[2] It is hard to say which of these texts and formulations is more central to Wesley on the subject in hand; he resorts to them again and again; he cleverly runs the content of these two verses together without worrying overmuch about exegetical exactitude. In unpacking Wesley's critical claims about the place of personal experience of God in knowledge of God, I shall provide a synthesis of his central proposals. The core claim at stake is a simple one: in responding to the gospel, the believer senses within his or her own heart the love of God that is manifest in the reconciling death of Jesus Christ for sinners. The challenge is to do justice to the way in which Wesley articulates this claim and the way in which he defends it aggressively against objections. I think there are at least four components in Wesley's vision that need to be recognized.

First, human beings in their sin are devoid of true knowledge of God. As a consequence of the fall, all human agents have lost the ability to perceive the truth about themselves and about God. Without radical divine assistance, we are malfunctioning cognitive agents in spiritual matters. Our rebellion against God, originating in Adam and handed down through the generations by way of original sin, has left us deeply disordered intellectually. Thus in and of ourselves we are no longer capable of perceiving the truth about God and ourselves.[3]

> After all that has been so plausibly written concerning "the innate idea of God"; after all that has been said of its being common to all men, in all ages and nations; it does not appear, that man has naturally any more idea of God than any of the beasts of the field; he has no knowledge

of God at all; no fear of God at all; neither is God in all his thoughts. Whatever change may afterwards be wrought, (whether by the grace of God, or by his own reflection, or by education,) he is, by nature, a mere Atheist.[4]

Given this predicament, we need the activity of grace to restore our capacities to their proper functions.

Second, in prevenient grace God irresistibly and universally restores in us the initial capacity to perceive the truth. This grace is manifest, for example, in conscience and in the initial desire to seek after God as something good and attractive. This action of God simply provides the preparatory work for what we really need, namely, the more direct action of God by the Holy Spirit to enable us to become aware of and see for ourselves what God has done for us in Jesus Christ. For this to happen we need either our damaged spiritual senses to be repaired or to receive new spiritual senses as an act of divine creation.[5] This gift of new senses is in fact the gift of faith by which we are acquitted or justified before God. Thus faith for Wesley is not just an act of trust on our part in response to the gospel; it is an act of trust generated by a God-given capacity to see and become aware of what God has done for us in the death of Jesus Christ. This is why Wesley loved Hebrews 11:1 so much. "Now faith is the assurance of things hoped for, the conviction of things not seen."

In deploying this text he is importing into it not just the idea that faith is a gift (a claim he develops in his exposition of Ephesians 2:4); he is also importing into the very idea of faith a cognitive component that is required by his doctrine of sin. In other words, faith is needed for the repair of our malfunctioning cognitive capacities in spiritual matters. The gift of faith restores the capacities for spiritual sight, proper spiritual hearing, or proper spiritual tasting of the reality of God. Without faith there is no perception, seeing, hearing or tasting of the things of God. Without faith, God's revelation in Christ or by the Spirit here and now remains totally opaque to us. We can hear but not hear and see but not see. With or without faith, the truth about God remains the same; his revelation is as real as anything can be; his speaking to us inwardly is a live option. However, without faith, given directly as a gift of the Holy Spirit, we remain as deaf as dodos. We simply do not have a well functioning receiver to pick up the extraordinary message that has been sent by God. We have to be taken back to the manufacturer for a repair job. We have to be taken into the hospital for cognitive surgery. Charles Wesley captures the issue brilliantly:

> The things unknown to feeble sense,
>   Unseen by reason's glimmering ray,
> With strong, commanding evidence,
>   Their heavenly origin display.
> Faith lends its realizing light:
>   The clouds disperse, the shadows fly;
> The Invisible appears in sight,
>   And God is seen by mortal eye![6]

Third, in turning to Romans 8:16 and the testimony of the Holy Spirit, Wesley develops further the role of God in bringing us to our senses and making us aware of the truth. With this verse the focus shifts from the repair of our senses to the direct speaking of God to us inwardly in our hearts: ". . . you have received a spirit of adoption. When we cry, 'Abba! Father!' it is that very Spirit bearing witness with our spirit that we are children of God. . . ." In this instance we shift from the repair-shop and the hospital to the law court. We are asked to think of the role of the Holy Spirit as that of a witness; we are invited to conceive of God speaking to us directly, so that when we hear the gospel we become aware of the love that is placarded in the death for our sins of Jesus Christ on the cross. Here, Wesley is after first-hand evidence supplied in the court of our hearts by God. At this point second-hand witnesses are essentially second-class witnesses; we really need to know what God knows; thus the Holy Spirit is understood as providing the best possible evidence for the issue at stake. As we move from bondage into adoption, the Holy Spirit speaks from within, bearing a witness or a testimony that tells us that we are the children of God. The effect of this action of the Spirit is that we can look up into the face of God and spontaneously call God "Abba, Father" just as Jesus did. We are now acquainted with God like a child acquainted with a loving father; we have filial knowledge of God; we have knowledge by acquaintance rather than by inference.

Fourth, it is precisely at this point that Wesley provides an explicit theory to undergird his claim of possessing knowledge of God. He insists that what is at stake is nothing less than perception of the divine. Just as by our ordinary physical senses we perceive the world around us, so by means of our spiritual senses we perceive the world of divine action. This faculty of spiritual sight is bedrock; either you possess it or you do not. For those who see, there is no need for external proof of what they see; for those who fail to see, there is nothing that can be done. Spiritual sight, just like ordinary sight, is a basic human capacity. Either you trust it or you do not. There is no deeper foundation below it to which we can appeal to secure its reliability. Wesley is very clear about this:

> But how may one who has the real witness in himself distinguish it from presumption? How, I pray, do you distinguish day from night? How do you distinguish light from darkness? Or the light of a star, or glimmering taper, from the light of the noonday sun? Is there not an inherent, obvious, essential difference between the one and the other? And do you not immediately and directly perceive that difference, provided your senses are rightly

disposed? In like manner, there is an inherent, essential difference between spiritual light and spiritual darkness; and between the light wherewith the sun of righteousness shines upon our heart, and that glimmering light which arises only from sparks of our own kindling. And this difference also is immediately and directly perceived, if our spiritual senses are rightly disposed.[7]

What do we do then with cases of illusion or delusion? What these cases show is that our senses are not infallible. In any particular case of sight, there are defeaters that undercut particular perceptual claims. Thus if I think I see an intruder in the house, this perceptual claim is secure as it stands. If on closer inspection I find out that it is my son coming in from orchestra practice, then the original claim is defeated. Or if I ask my daughter and she points out that I am mistaking a shadow for an intruder, the claim is defeated. This example only shows, however, that the original claim is corrigible; it does not undercut the reliance on sense perception. Indeed the original claim is only defeated because of other instances of perception, so the reliability of the sense remains intact. It is likewise with spiritual perception. The claim to have seen the truth about God through the inner witness stays intact unless it is defeated. One way to defeat it is to draw attention to the absence of the testimony of our own spirits, that is, to draw attention to the fact that the fruits of the Holy Spirit are conspicuously absent from our lives. If someone claims to have the inner witness but their lives are marked by anger, fear, cruelty, and the like, then he or she is deluded. Thus Wesley has in hand ways of withdrawing the claim that someone has come to gain filial knowledge of God, but he does so in a way that keeps the original reliance on the spiritual senses intact.

At this point we can readily bring Wesley's claims about sin, faith, and the inner witness of the Holy Spirit into conversation with material in the epistemology of theology that has received attention over the last thirty years. Technically the language may differ, but there are striking representations of Wesley's proposals available. It is enough for our purposes here to make the relevant connections.

The first three themes I identified above (cognitive malfunction, faith, and the inner witness) have been deployed in the work of Alvin Plantinga. Plantinga's project is to develop a general theory of knowledge that makes proper function its heartbeat. Knowledge is constituted by warrant. Warrant in turn is made available when our beliefs are produced by cognitive faculties functioning properly (subject to no dysfunction) in a cognitive environment that is appropriate for our cognitive faculties, according to a design plan that is successfully aimed at truth.[8] In the case of religious belief, what this means is that we are so designed by God that through a *sensus divinitatis* we form theistic beliefs and thereby gain natural knowledge of God. Unfortunately this natural knowledge is "compromised, weakened, reduced, smothered, overlaid or impeded by sin and its consequences."[9] In response to this God instituted a plan of salvation through the life, death, and resurrection of his Son, the second person of the Trinity. God then saw to it that this good news was enshrined in Scripture. Beyond that God sent the Holy Spirit to make it possible for us to come to believe the great truths of the gospel.

> By virtue of the Holy Spirit in the hearts of those to whom faith is given, the ravages of sin (including the cognitive damage) are repaired, gradually or suddenly, to a lesser or greater extent. Furthermore, it is by virtue of the activity of the Holy Spirit that Christians come to grasp, believe, accept, endorse, and rejoice in the truth of the great things of the gospel. It is thus by virtue of this activity that the Christian believes that "in Christ, God was reconciling the

world to himself, not counting men's sins against them."
(2 Corinthians 5:19)[10]

As in the case of Wesley, this knowledge is corrigible; defeaters can undermine it.

We can see clearly here the fascinating parallels between Wesley and Plantinga. Both reject the notion of the need for natural theology as being essential to the rationality of Christian belief. Both are interested in the great truths of the gospel rather than mere theism. Both insist on cognitive dysfunction through sin and cognitive repair through the work of the Holy Spirit. Both see faith as a cognitive gift related intimately to regeneration. Both have a critical place for Scripture. Both recognize the problem of evil but do not see it as undermining the rationality of Christian belief. Both seek to rebut defeaters against classical Christian belief. Both can handle degrees of certainty. Both allow that there can be good arguments for the Christian faith without making those arguments foundational or essential to our spiritual and intellectual welfare. They do, however, differ dramatically at one point: Wesley but not Plantinga makes much of perception of the divine.

This latter theme of Wesley (perception of the divine) shows up prominently in the work of William P. Alston.[11] It is tempting to see this as stemming from Alston's initial (if nominal) formation in Methodism before he abandoned the Christian faith.[12] However, such biographical speculation is beside the point here. What Alston posits is that we can rightly construe much Christian experience of God in terms of perception of the divine. Thus he begins, as Wesley does, with the potential analogies between ordinary sense perception and perception of God. In earlier efforts to run the analogies the common strategy was simply to think of one mode of perception and then look for its manifestations in various modes. The problem for religious experience was immediately apparent. The disanalogies between sense perception and perception of God were so obvious that the veridicality of religious perception quickly came into question. There is no corroboration from the other senses; there are significant disagreements, contested background beliefs in place, and so on. Alston's formulation of the argument, however, reworked the claim so that this kind of quick dismissal was rebutted. His strategy was simple and subtle. Thus he posited the idea of a doxastic practice, that is, the idea that our beliefs arise out of a network of practices that have their own input-output systems and their own overrider systems. This allowed him to work out a theory of perception of the divine that did not have to be matched one-to-one as in the case of sense perception. What matters is that both ordinary perception and perception of the divine share a common epistemic structure; hence reliability applies to both.

> The analogies between CMP [Christian mystical perceptual doxastic practice] and SP [sense perceptual doxastic practice] that are needed to yield the conclusion that CMP is rationally engaged in and rationally taken to be reliable if SP is, are the ones just noted: being a full-fledged socially established doxastic practice with distinctive output functions, having a functioning overrider system, the lack of sufficient reasons to take the practice as unreliable, and a significant degree of self-support.[13]

But the modalities of each structure are different, so it is imperialistic and question begging to insist that the exact modalities that apply in the case of sense perception have to be in place in the case of perception of the divine.

Wesley, of course, does not begin to display the intellectual horsepower visible in Alston. Alston, however, makes available to the modern Wesleyan a way of unpacking Wesley's claims about perception of the divine that are fruitful.[14] Both treat perception as a bedrock capacity that we either trust or not. Both aggressively pursue the parallels between sense perception and perception of the divine. Both put enormous emphasis on the importance of social and communal practices as critical in coming to perception of the divine. Both allow for defeaters and rebuttals. Both are keen to deploy cumulative case arguments.[15] And both are committed to a robust place not just for Scripture but also for special divine revelation in the justification of religious belief. They differ in that Wesley has personally next to no confidence in natural theology, while Alston is more than ready to draw on a revised natural theology as part of a cumulative case argument for the Christian faith.

They also differ in that at one level Wesley puts enormous store by the evidence of perception of the divine. For him the inner witness of the Holy Spirit was extremely important:

> This is the privilege of all the children of God, and without this we can never retain a steady peace, nor avoid perplexing doubts and fears. But when we have once received this Spirit of adoption, this peace which passeth all understanding, and which expels all painful doubts and fear, will keep our hearts and minds in Christ Jesus.[16]

Thus for Wesley, filial knowledge of God was not just one more piece of evidence among others; it had a privileged place in his epistemology.[17] This comes out especially clearly in his comments on his father's death:

> My father did not die unacquainted with the faith of the Gospel, of the primitive Christians, or of our first Reformers; the same which, by the grace of God, I preach, and which is just as new as Christianity. What he experienced before, I know not; but I know that during his last illness, which continued eight months, he enjoyed a clear sense of his acceptance with God. I heard him express it more than once, although at that time I understood him not.

The inward witness, son, the inward witness, said he to
me, that is the proof, the strongest proof, of Christianity. And when I asked him, (the time of his change drawing nigh,) Sir, are you in much pain? he answered aloud
with a smile, God does chasten me with pain, yea, all my
bones with strong pain; but I thank Him for all, I bless
Him for all, I love Him for all! I think the last words he
spoke, when I had just commended his soul to God, were,
Now you have done all. And with the same serene, cheer-
ful countenance he fell asleep, without one struggle, or
sigh, or groan. I cannot therefore doubt but the Spirit of
God bore an inward witness with his spirit, that he was a
child of God.[18]

Neither Plantinga nor Alston develop this line of argument, so Wesley looks as if he is out of tune with the contemporary discussion at this point. However, help is at hand in
the recent work of Paul Moser, the third contemporary phi-
losopher I wish to connect with Wesley's proposals. Interact-
ing with recent work in the philosophy of religion but going
beyond it, Moser has explored precisely the theme that was
so dear to the heart of Wesley, namely filial knowledge of
God.[19] My aim at this stage is to pull back the veil and get a
glimpse of the bigger picture.

One way into Moser's project is to see it as starting with
a pivotal comment on the nature of knowledge of God. If God
is as we think he is, then knowledge of God should not be
divorced from moral transformation. "As morally impecca-
ble, the true God must work in human history to encourage
free human agents to seek God's kind of moral excellence via
knowing God and God's goodness."[20] Thus the robust theism
of the Jewish and Christian traditions undercuts our setting
conditions on how we must come to know God from an intellectual point of view. We must allow God to come to us in a
way that meets God's agenda for holiness. In the Christian

tradition God has come to us in his Son and through the Spirit in a way that involves in the end a transforming filial knowledge of God.

> Filial knowledge of God is *reconciling* personal knowledge whereby we enter into an appropriate *child-parent* relationship with God. Such knowledge is personally transforming, not impersonally abstract or morally impotent. It is communicated by God's *personal* Spirit in a way that demands full life-commitment. Knowledge of a robustly personal God requires *personal* evidence (such as evidence of a will), not mere nonpersonal reasons. So this knowledge is not just a true conclusion endorsed on the basis of warranted inference. Sound argument, however warranted, does not itself offer the kind of personal *power* central to Jewish-Christian theism: namely, God's personal power of self-giving love as our liberator, motivator, and transformer. Filial knowledge of God entails our commitment to participate gratefully in God's purposes with all that we are and have. It is thus purposeful knowledge as loving and obedient discipleship toward a personal agent, not mere intellectual assent. It is inherently person-relational.[21]

Very naturally human beings resist this kind of move on God's part. Hence if there is to be true personal knowledge of God, God himself has to supply it in our hearts:

> God must work as an internal, convicting Authority and Assurer who makes people qualitatively new, in a way that makes Cartesian certainty look sterile and weak. . . . God's Spirit must witness with our spirits that we are indeed children of God, that God is indeed our gracious Father. As Reconciler, God must offer a unique kind of personal assurance, as a gift and not as a tool for abusive human control. God, after all, has no need of a cognitive

sledgehammer. This fits well with robust theism as well as God's personal character of humble love.[22]

To reject the divine strategy in bringing us to knowledge of God is to commit cognitive idolatry, that is, to lay down the law to God as to how God must work. We should not be surprised that God hides from those with such hubris. This is not a matter of divine anger, but an entirely appropriate response from God, for God is committed to our moral transformation. Moreover, without an attitude of openness we may be blind to the reality of God. Knowledge of God is not a spectator sport. "God reveals God on God's gracious terms, as a gift, rather than on our self-crediting terms."[23] Hence, while we must personally seek God and give up any idea of earning God's favor, God is sovereign and will come to us in a way that meets our moral and spiritual condition. Esoteric philosophical reasoning may take us away from God rather than toward God. Moreover, while God is perfectly capable of performing signs and miracles, these may entertain us rather than bring us to faith. What we need most is the presence of God's morally transforming love; and this is

> the central *epistemic*, or *evidential*, foundation for filial knowledge of God. Such love is a foundational source of knowledge of God (cf. Colossians 2:2; 1 Corinthians 8:2-3). It is real evidence of God's reality and presence. This love is a matter of personal intervention by God and the basis of a personal relationship with God. It is the distinctive presence of a personal God. So the filial knowledge in question rests on morally transforming divine love that produces a loving character in genuine children of God, even if at times such people obstruct God's transformation. This transformation *happens to one*, in part, and thus is neither purely self-made nor simply the byproduct of a self-help strategy.[24]

Moser even deploys two of Wesley's favorite scriptural texts on the topic.

> God's self-revelation of transforming love will take us beyond mere historical and scientific probabilities to a firm foundation of *personal acquaintance* with God. As Paul remarks, in our sincerely crying out "Abba, Father" to God (note the Jesus-inspired filial content of this cry), God's Spirit confirms to our spirit that we are indeed children of God (Romans 8:16). We thereby receive God's personal assurance of our filial relationship with God. This assurance is more robust than any kind of theoretical certainty offered by philosophers or theologians. It liberates a person from dependence merely on the quagmire of speculation, hypothesis-formation, probabilistic inference, or guesswork about God. Such assurance yields a distinctive kind of grounded firm confidence in God unavailable elsewhere. God thus merits credit even for proper human confidence in God (cf. Ephesians 2:8).[25]

I trust that I have supplied enough to show the deep connection that exists here between Wesley and Moser. Both ransack Scripture for epistemic material. Both are open to but wary of speculative, philosophical knowledge of God. Both insist that we can have knowledge of God without having complete explanations about the nature and character of God. Both draw attention to the themes of blindness and sight in coming to knowledge of God. Both put much store by the promises of God. "'When you search for me, you will find me; if you seek me with all your heart, I will let you find me, says the Lord. . . .' (Jeremiah 29:13-14; cf. Matthew 7:7-8)."[26] And above all, both think that filial knowledge of God is of the highest authority in the epistemology of theology.

> The proof of God is, finally, in morally serious testing. Seek aright, then, and you will find incomparable knowledge

and new life as well. What's more, the joyous firstfruits of the eventual redemption (where God will wipe away every tear and death and suffering shall be no more) are already apparent in our sadly broken world—if only we have eyes to see and ears to hear. When our diagnosing God gives way to our thanking and even praising God, we shall know for sure that we have been made new. The Jewish-Christian God is, in the end, hidden only in God's unique superhuman love for all.[27]

Thus far I have sought to do two things. First, I have summarized the nature and place of personal experience of God in Wesley. Second, I have shown how Wesley's views are by no means archaic or idiosyncratic. In fact, nearly every single one of his concerns is readily visible in some of the very best work in recent philosophy of religion. Yet, in closing, we need to stand back and answer an obvious objection or worry. Is not all this complicated work in philosophy a terrible distraction? Would Wesley really want to be associated with such complicated paraphernalia as proper functioning, *sensus divinitatis*, doxastic practices, knowledge by acquaintance, filial knowledge of God, and the like? Can we not just get on with preaching the gospel and ignore all this technical baggage? There are really two questions here, so let me work with both.

As to what Wesley would want, well, of course, he is dead and gone. On his account of life after death, we get to continue our ministry for good with the holy angels, so he may be whispering in our dreams and cheering us on from the sidelines, for all we know.[28] We cannot say for sure whether he would approve of what we are doing. However, we can say this: Wesley himself, as we have seen here, is deeply interested in making sense of how we know God, so I would claim his patronage in general terms.

Furthermore, we now know that Wesley in his day was deeply dependent on the work of Christian philosophers in that they created intellectual space for his own work in evangelism and in unpacking a unique vision of the Christian life. The Christian faith had been under severe assault from intellectuals within and without the church in his day. The rebuttals to such assaults in Joseph Butler, William Law, Bishop Berkeley, William Warburton, and others was extremely important in clearing the decks for what Wesley had to do. When time allowed, Wesley added his own aid in this work. The intellectual opposition to robust forms of the Christian faith is as real today (if not more so) as it was in the eighteenth century. In our work of evangelism, catechesis, and spiritual formation, we need rebuttals to such opposition as much as Wesley did then. We all need good intellectual background music to sing our evangelistic songs of praise and invitation. I consider it a great privilege to be alive at a time when we have in hand the extraordinary intellectual resources that have emerged over the last forty years. It is high time Methodists and Wesleyans come to terms with them.

Secondly, it is clear that our ministry in the church depends first and foremost on God, that is, on the gospel, on the great canonical heritage of the church, and on the mysterious testimony of the Holy Spirit. Unfasten these and we are destined to death and extinction. In this respect Methodism as a worldwide movement has sinned from time to time (sinned even grievously from time to time), so we need to repent and be about the tough task of retrieval and renewal.[29] If this philosophical work undermines the first-order life of the church, then we should set it aside and seek the face of the Lord afresh. We should go into mourning, take upon us sackcloth and ashes, hide away in monasteries and places of retreat, and fast and pray until the Lord has mercy upon us and pours out a new Pentecost on his people. So let us be clear about the proper ordering of the life of faith. With that settled and said, I can now press home my final comments.

In this philosophical work we are not running away from the gospel or from God; we are seeking to come to terms intellectually with the presence of God in our midst. We are about the business of loving God with all our minds. In this we stand with Wesley and the whole history of the church across the ages. There is a natural harmony between our experience of God and intellectual theorizing. Our filial experience of God, however fleet and faint, is drawn into and integrated into our lives as a whole.

Furthermore, our convictions about knowledge of God have a bearing on the practice of ministry. Given Wesley's considered views on the critical importance of preaching, spiritual guidance, and the means of grace in fostering filial knowledge of God, he organized the life of his movement accordingly. So the issues that swirl in and around faith and reason are not abstract, impractical matters; they have a bearing on the practice of ministry. If we take what I have outlined here seriously, then we shall look on our practices not just pragmatically but theologically and spiritually.

Finally, can we not believe that the Holy Spirit will gather up even these efforts and use them to foster knowledge of the Triune God? Even in this work on faith and reason we can seek the guidance of the Holy Spirit. Even in this work we can hope and pray that God will draw people to himself. Even in this work we can come to a deeper knowledge of God in our own personal journey from sin to salvation and from time into eternity.

Chapter 3

Faith and the Power of God

In his Aldersgate experience John Wesley was convinced that at least three things had happened to him. He had come to experience the fulfillment of divine promise that had been preached to him by Peter Böhler and the Moravians. He had come to perceive the love of God for himself, so much so that he could with integrity and sincerity call God "Abba, Father." And he had come to experience the power of God, giving him a measure of victory over sin that he had not known before. Wesley was not content, however, to leave his Aldersgate experience in merely autobiographical terms. He was also interested in unpacking how these experiences constituted evidence for the truth of the Christian faith.

Two kinds of arguments surface when we attend to what is at stake. First, there is the argument from the fulfillment of divine promises. I put the argument formally in this fashion: If many people have satisfied to a significant extent the conditions laid down for a sense of pardon from the guilt and power of sin, and if they, or a large proportion of them, then receive such a sense of pardon and power, this provides us with evidence for the truth of the claim that this promise was indeed made by a being with the wherewithal and the will to make good on that promise. The argument can be readily reformulated to include the second element of Wesley's experience. Therefore we can run it not just in terms of the promise to experience pardon and power, but also in terms of the promise to perceive the love of God for oneself. If many people have satisfied to a significant extent the conditions laid down for perceiving the love of God for themselves, and if they, or a large proportion of them, then receive such perception of the love of God for themselves, this provides us with evidence for the truth of the claim that this promise was indeed made by a being who has the wherewithal and the will to make good on that promise.

Second, there is the argument from the nature of faith or from the inner witness of the Holy Spirit, where the heart of the matter is captured by the claim to perceive God. In this instance Wesley unpacked the argument as a quasi-empirical argument in which perception of the divine was secured as reliable by exploring the nature of ordinary sensory perception. Thus Wesley held that if one accepted the reliability of sense perception of the natural world, then one had good reason to accept the reality of spiritual perception of the invisible world. Spiritual perception of the divine provided good *prima facie* evidence for claims about the nature of the divine. This perception is not incorrigible; it can be overridden in various ways. But the default position is that it is reliable until we have good reason to believe otherwise.

We turn now to a third argument that showed up in Wesley's writings in and around Aldersgate, namely, the argument from the power of God at work in our lives. We can also, in fact, capture this argument in terms of the fulfillment of divine promise. Indeed our formulation has already caught this in the argument from divine promise, for that argument centers on sensing divine pardon for sin and *divine power over sin.* However, I want in this chapter to explore a different network of arguments from divine power, namely, an argument from conspicuous sanctity or holiness in others and an argument from what Wesley would have called the extraordinary gifts of the Holy Spirit. The evidence in this case goes beyond any signs of grace in our own lives and focuses on the power of God to produce holiness and supernatural phenomena. While I shall go beyond what Wesley has to say, especially in formally identifying the logic of the argument, I want to report that what Wesley does have to say, particularly on the argument from charismatic phenomena, is absolutely fascinating.[1]

What is the argument from divine power? Essentially it is an abductive argument to the best explanation. In encountering conspicuous sanctity and purported direct divine action in charismatic phenomena, we find that the phenomena involved are best explained in terms of the activity of the Holy Spirit. Thus the phenomena provide relevant and persuasive evidence of the reality of God. The phenomena make sense if we believe in God; otherwise they remain unexplained and anomalous. The evidence does not constitute proof, but it does carry weight in its own right; it can therefore play a legitimate part in cumulative case arguments for the truth of Christian doctrine.

Before I give details, it should be noted that we are dealing here with phenomena that often play a critical role in conversion. It is generally recognized that many people come to faith not because of propositional evidence but because they have come to know someone who loves the socks off them or someone who generally exhibits a life of holiness. Equally, we know lots of cases where people are brought significantly toward faith because of the manifestation of the power of God in miracles, healing, exorcisms, prophecies, visions, speaking in tongues, and words of knowledge. What we want to know is why this is the case. Is this simply a matter of emotional or psychological impact? Or is there something intellectual and cognitive at stake? Wesley was very clear that the latter was the case.[2] What we are doing in what ensues is following his lead on the matter.

The evidence from conspicuous sanctity arises in this way. Suppose we meet someone who exhibits the kind of loving, self-sacrificing sanctity that catches our attention and takes our breath away. Due to this encounter our skepticism about God may be checked, and we may well be drawn to believe in God. Here is how Wesley made this point:

> The beauty of holiness, of that inward man of the heart which is renewed after the image of God, cannot but strike every eye which God hath opened, every enlightened understanding. The ornament of a meek, humble, loving spirit will at least excite the approbation of all those who are capable in any degree of discerning spiritual good and evil. From the hour men begin to emerge out of the darkness which covers the giddy, unthinking world, they cannot but perceive how desirable a thing it is to be thus transformed into the likeness of him that created us. *This inward religion bears the shape of God so visibly impressed upon it that a soul must be wholly immersed in flesh and blood when he can doubt of its divine original.*[3]

So let's suppose the skeptic or the agnostic meets a saint; or they encounter someone who exhibits the kind of life that Wesley expounds on a host of occasions as real Christianity, entire sanctification, unspotted holiness, the recovery of the image of God, and so on. How is the skeptic or agnostic to understand this phenomenon? More generally, we ask, what is the cause of this phenomenon? The saint has an immediate response to this question. We are to see this phenomenon (he or she insists) as causally brought about by the grace of God. Thus the phenomenon is to be explained in terms of the power of God. It is certainly not a matter of his or her own doing. As Paul puts the issue succinctly: "But by the grace of God I am what I am. . . . I worked harder than any of them—though it was not I, but the grace of God that is with me."[4] The best explanation is furnished by the avowals of the agent that this is not his or her doing, it is the grace of God. In the absence of a better explanation, we have evidence of the agency of God.

But why should we accept this description and explanation? Perhaps the saint is lying to us. However, this will not work simply because we would not grant the initial description of sanctity if the person involved was a liar. Saints who persistently lie are not saints; we would have to drastically alter our initial impression or description. So this route is not very promising; we have no good reason to change our initial impression or description. The critic, then, will have to try another tack. Perhaps there are possible natural causes at hand. The saint's goodness (it will be said) is attributable to various psychological and sociological factors that *on their own* explain the phenomena of sanctity. However, while this is not an impossible way out, it is subject to serious objection. First, we need a specific, relevant psychological or sociological explanation for the phenomena in question; it is not enough to wave a hand with mere possibilities. As yet we do not have such explanations available to us; certainly I know of none. Second, even if we did have explanations that invoked the relevant, specific factors at hand, we would need an additional argument to show that these are *the only factors* at work. This kind of reductionist move is notoriously difficult to secure; especially so when conceptually it is clear that the agency of God can work in, with, and through the natural order. Hence in the absence of a compelling alternative, the robust theist has in hand a compelling case to accept the best explanation available, namely, an explanation in terms of the power of God. The theist has a good abductive argument for Christian doctrine from the existence of conspicuous sanctity. As Wesley noted, "This inward religion bears the shape of God so visibly impressed upon it that a soul must be wholly immersed in flesh and blood when he can doubt of its divine original."[5]

So much for the argument from conspicuous sanctity. How now shall we run the argument from charismatic activity?[6] Wesley gives explicit attention to this argument in his remarkable response to the essay of Conyers Middleton entitled "Free Inquiry." Middleton had essentially argued that there was no good argument for the existence of charismatic phenomena in the history of the church beyond the apostolic age.[7] Wesley was clearly annoyed by the essay, for he took time out of his busy schedule to write an extended reply. Middleton's strategy took the form of refuting all claims to extraordinary spiritual phenomena across the whole history of the church, right up to the New Testament period. He deployed a kind of nuclear strike that would in one stroke eliminate supernatural phenomena in the history of the church. His nuclear strike took the form of an argument against historical testimony. Wesley accurately summarized the move in this way: "The credibility of facts lies open to the trial of our reason and senses. But the credibility of witnesses depends on a variety of principles wholly concealed from us. And though in many cases it may reasonably be presumed, yet in none can it be certainly known."[8] Middleton's crucial point here is that given that we can never know if historical witnesses are reliable, we should be agnostic regarding the value of their testimony.

Wesley smelled a nest of rats lurking below the surface; he sent in his intellectual ferrets to bring them out into the open. He rightly noted that Middleton's whole argument on the nature of testimony would in time undercut all historical investigation. "Sir, will you retract this, or defend it? If you defend, and can prove, as well as assert it, then farewell the credit of all history, not only sacred but profane."[9]

Middleton has clearly proved too much. He has undermined the testimony to miracle by undermining all historical testimony. Wesley also astutely recognized that you could not allow skeptical historical investigation to reach back into the second century and then suddenly cry halt when it knocked at the door of the first century, that is, to Jesus and the apostles. In the central section of his rejoinder he took on the specific arguments of Middleton as those related to matters of fact and the quality of the patristic witnesses. Here Wesley narrowed the field to the first three centuries, digging in resolutely to defend his great heroes of the faith prior to the fall of the church with Constantine in the fourth century.[10] What is of interest here is how Wesley weighed the arguments from charismatic phenomena and then made a fascinating epistemological comment.

Wesley worked through the evidence for Christian belief as it related to miracles, healing, exorcisms, prophecies, visions, speaking in tongues, and words of knowledge. It suffices in this context to see what he does in the case of divine healings. Middleton focused on cases where miraculous healing occurred in the context of anointing with oil. Hence the form of the argument is clearly an argument for the best explanation. If a healing occurs after anointing with oil (and the implied invocation of the Holy Spirit), then an obvious way to explain the healing is in terms of the activity of God. Certainly this is how the robust Christian theist might read the situation. The phenomenon of healing is best explained by seeing it as caused by the Holy Spirit.

Middleton challenged this initially by positing a natural explanation, that is, by attributing the healing to the natural efficacy of the oil itself. Wesley was unconvinced. "Be pleased to try how many you can cure thus, that are blind, deaf, dumb, or paralytic; and experience, if not philosophy, will teach you, the oil has no such natural efficacy as this."[11] Middleton then tried another explanation: the whole matter was a cheat from the beginning to end. Wesley found the arguments deployed in defense of this option equally unconvincing. Whatever else we may say, the witnesses in the first three centuries were not cheats; there were too many of good standing to dismiss in this cavalier fashion. Then Middleton tried out another possible explanation: maybe we are dealing with cases of spontaneous cures. Then negatively, he argued that unless we know precisely the real bounds between nature and miracle, we will not be able to posit that the best explanation is one given in terms of divine agency. Here is Wesley's reply:

> . . . although we grant, that some recover, even in seemingly desperate cases; and, that we do not know, in any case, the precise bounds between nature and miracle; yet it does not follow, therefore I cannot be assured there ever was a miracle of healing in the world. To explain this by instance: I do not precisely know how far nature may go in healing, that is, restoring sight to, the blind; yet this I assuredly know, that if a man born blind is restored to sight by a word, this is not nature, but miracle. And to such a story, well attested, all reasonable men will pay the highest regard.[12]

Even without an explicit criterion, Wesley insisted that when we attend to specific, particular examples of healing, they are convincingly read as miracles.

Wesley's argument was a modest one. If healing occurs in response to anointing with oil, provided we are dealing with witnesses that we have no reason to challenge *ab initio*, and provided there are no good specific, naturalistic explanations available, and provided we have no other defeaters, then we have evidence of the power of God at work in history.[13] *Mutatis mutandis* this argument can be applied to the whole gamut of charismatic phenomena in the history of the church.

Yet Wesley did not stop there in his analysis. In the concluding section of his response to Middleton, he made two supplementary comments that are exceptionally interesting. First, he clearly preferred the evidence from the fulfillment of divine promises and the evidence from perception of the divine to the argument from charismatic phenomena. Here is a felicitous restatement of the two arguments (that of promise and perception of the divine) put together.

> The faith by which the promise is attained is represented by Christianity, as a power wrought by the Almighty in an immortal spirit, inhabiting a house of clay, to see through that veil into the world of spirits, into things invisible and eternal; a power to discern those things which with eyes of flesh and blood no man hath seen or can see, either by reason of their nature, which (though they surround us on every side) is not perceivable by these gross senses; or by reason of their distance, as being yet afar off in the bosom of eternity.[14]

It was this kind of evidence rather than historical or traditional evidence from charismatic phenomena that Wesley preferred to advance.

Even then, Wesley did not cast aside what he terms here "traditional evidence." He thinks that there is merit in it: "I do not undervalue traditional evidence. Let it have its place and its due honour. It is highly serviceable in its kind, and in its degree."[15] So why did he think this sort of evidence was inferior? He had two reasons. The first focused on the issue of time:

> It is generally supposed, that traditional evidence is weakened by length of time; as it must necessarily pass through so many hands, in a continued succession of ages. But no length of time can possibly affect the strength of this internal evidence. It is equally strong, equally new,

through the course of seventeen hundred years. It passes now, even as it has done from the beginning, directly from God into the believing soul. Do you suppose time will ever dry up this stream? O no! It shall never be cut off: *Labitur et labetur in omne volubilis aevum*. [It flows on and will forever flow.][16]

The second reason had to do with the issue of complexity.

Traditional evidence is of an extremely complicated nature, necessarily including so many and so various considerations, that only men of a strong and clear understanding can be sensible of its full force. On the contrary, how plain and simple is this; and how level to the lowest capacity! Is not this the sum: One thing I know; I was blind, but now I see? An argument so plain, that a peasant, a woman, a child, may feel all its force.[17]

Essentially, then, Wesley thought that historical evidence is weakened by time; and the evidence is much too complicated compared to the contemporaneity and simplicity of the inward evidence. These are fascinating moves.

Second, Wesley made an intriguing theological and cultural comment to fill out his analysis.

I have sometimes been almost inclined to believe, that the wisdom of God has, in most later ages, permitted the external evidence of Christianity to be more or less clogged and incumbered for this very end, that men (of reflection especially) might not altogether rest there, but be constrained to look into themselves also, and attend to the light shining in their hearts. Nay, it seems (if it may be allowed for us to pry so far into the reasons of the divine dispensations) that, particularly in this age, God suffers all kind of objections to be raised against the traditional evidence of Christianity, that men of understanding, though unwilling to give it up, yet, at the same time they defend this evidence, may not rest the whole strength of their cause thereon, but seek a deeper and firmer support for it. Without this I cannot but doubt, whether they can long maintain their cause; whether, if they do not obey the loud call of God, and lay far more stress than they have hitherto done on this internal evidence of Christianity, they will not, one after another, give up the external, and (in heart at least) go over to those whom they are now contending with; so that in a century or two the people of England will be fairly divided into real Deists and real Christians.[18]

What Wesley was doing here in this little piece of cultural analysis was welcoming the assault on the traditional historical arguments for Christian doctrine. He displayed at this point a remarkable historical sense of the development of Christian thought as under the care of providence. He was happy to let Middleton's skeptical rats eat away at the traditional arguments because this may then create the space for a proper appreciation of the truly significant evidence in favor of Christian doctrine, namely, the evidence from the fulfillment of divine promises and the evidence from perception of the divine. Indeed Wesley went so far as to use Middleton's skeptical arguments as a way of waking nominal Christians from their dogmatic slumbers and forcing them to decide between Deism and real Christianity. Once the arguments from the Deists and rationalists have had their effect, God may have a real chance of getting through to them.

> Go on, gentlemen, and prosper. Shame these nominal Christians out of that poor superstition which they call Christianity. Reason, rally, laugh them out of their dead, empty forms, void of spirit, of faith, of love. Convince them, that such mean pageantry (for such it manifestly is, if there is nothing in the heart correspondent with the outward show) is absolutely unworthy, you need not say

of God, but even of any man that is endued with common understanding. Show them, that while they are endeavouring to please God thus, they are only beating the air. Know your time; press on; push your victories, till you have conquered all that know not God. And then He, whom neither they nor you know now, shall rise and gird himself with strength, and go forth in his almighty love, and sweetly conquer you all together.[19]

This was surely a remarkable and daring comment; it shows a side of Wesley that we do not often see, that is, a subtlety that often escaped him.

Let me begin my own commentary and final assessment of Wesley's argument by noting the obvious relevance of Wesley's cultural comment to what has happened in the two hundred years since his death. To his astonishment Wesley may well have gotten his wishes. On the one hand, the tough rationalist and empiricist critique of the last two hundred years of robust forms of Christianity has been both persistent and effective in the West. We can legitimately read the decline of the Christian faith in Europe as intimately related to the brilliant attacks on the Christian gospel that developed in a host of forms in the nineteenth and twentieth century. The story is a complex one, but it is accurate to say that one crucial part of the attack has focused on the intelligibility and rationality of believing what Wesley called the "traditional evidence." Historical and philosophical arguments against Wesley's robust form of theism litter the landscape, many of them developed by historical critics and professional theologians in the name of truth and intellectual virtue.[20]

On the other hand, while much of the argument against such evidence remains in place, the acids of postmodernity and the unexpected resurgence of Christian philosophy within the analytic tradition have called into question the confidence that once marked this kind of work. These, of course, are strange bedfellows, for analytic philosophers and postmodern critics are not usually seen within earshot of each other. Yet the combined effect of their work is beginning to bite deep into the standard opposition of charismatic phenomena. More importantly, we now have the extraordinary development of forms of Christianity that unapologetically lead in their witness with appeals to the present power of God in our lives. In the West this occurrence is represented by a resurgence of some forms of Evangelicalism and by the appearance of the Charismatic Movement and Pentecostalism. Outside the West it is represented by the extraordinary growth of forms of Christianity that unashamedly give testimony to personal encounter with God and that look to signs and wonders as authenticating evidence for the truth of the gospel. It almost looks as if God has fulfilled Wesley's aspiration noted above: "And then He, whom neither they nor you know now, shall rise and gird himself with strength, and go forth in his almighty love, and sweetly conquer you all together." If this is true, I hope Father Wesley (in keeping with his workaholic eschatology) has been able to eavesdrop and lend a hand.

Given this radically altered landscape we now need to go back and see if Wesley's views need revision. Recall what his central claims were. The appeal to the power of God in charismatic phenomena has epistemic weight, but compared to the appeal to fulfillment of divine promises and to inward perception of the divine, it is too remote and too complicated to be of value today. Thus we should let it fade into the background for a time and work off the stronger and simpler forms of evidence available to the ordinary believer now. Is Wesley right here?

His first argument (the argument from distance) no longer holds in our contemporary situation. We have a wealth of charismatic phenomena available to us in the contemporary church. Hence the argument from distance or from the weakening of time is no longer available to him. Put more positively, we should not make the concession that Wesley did to Middleton. Of course, the relevant material can be dismissed (as it often is) without examination as credulity and superstition; but this is simply (as Wesley might say) beating the air with words. It is the mere *ipse dixi* of the critic, rather than the rational examination of pertinent evidence. We can and should expect this kind of intellectual hostility, and I shall return to this at the end.

Wesley's second argument (the argument from complexity) is also extremely weak when we explore it with care. The argument from charismatic phenomena is as complicated or as simple as the argument from personal experience of God. Wesley was clearly well aware of the complexity at issue in the case of the argument from perception of the divine. He knew that while the claim is initially "simple," that is, it is an appeal to inward perception of the divine, the articulation and defense of this evidence was complicated. Many of his readers would have failed to get the point of his analogy between sense perception and perception of the divine. The work of the last generation in, say, figures like Plantinga and Alston, makes it clear that the theist does not have a "simple" argument. Providing an account of the logic of the argument and overturning defeaters is inescapable in any development of what is at stake. The argument from charismatic phenomena is complicated and none the worse for that. All of these arguments are complicated in the sense that articulating them takes effort and thought.

However, this does not mean that the force of these arguments is not in a real sense obvious to the ordinary believer or to the genuine seeker of truth. Nor does it mean that they should not have real force in our lives; they are indeed evidence that strikes us intuitively and cogently. In all of these arguments, the evidence is more often than not tacit rather than articulated; it is implicit rather than explicit; it is person-relative rather than universal. The force of all these arguments tends to strike us as fundamentally similar in this respect. There is no relevant difference in logic between them; hence one is not to be preferred over the other. So Wesley was mistaken in his assessment of their relative merits. In exalting the case for the fulfillment of divine promises and inward perception of the divine, he too readily undersold the value of the argument from divine power. The good news is that once his mistakes are removed, we strengthen rather than weaken his overall case. We need, that is, to retrieve and restate the argument from charismatic phenomena.

Yet someone might still want to say that the evidence from charismatic phenomena is altogether more sensational and therefore wobblier than the evidence from promise fulfillment and inward divine perception. The more spectacular the evidence, the more abnormal it will appear, and therefore the more precarious it will appear to the seeker of truth. So should we not leave aside charismatic phenomena for fear that we may invite charges of credulity and superstition? If we do not do so, it might be said, we lose before we even begin.

I do not find this at all convincing. Precisely the same worry besets the argument from fulfillment of divine promises, inward perception, and conspicuous sanctity. Sometimes these take the form of what we can only call spectacular phenomena. Wesley himself knew this in that he was aware that Christian conversion (a term we may use here as a summary for what was at stake) could indeed be spectacular. Equally, it is often the case that the saints exhibit sanctity that can only be described as spectacular. On the other side, much of what counts as charismatic phenomena is far from spectacular. In my own experience as a witness of divine healing, exorcism, and speaking in tongues, for example, the evidence was quiet and unsensational. I can, of course, with a bit of blarney dress it up to look spectacular; but this is a rhetorical matter rather than straight description. The accounts of charismatic phenomena are generally made out to be spectacular because they are so little known and because we are used to anecdotal evidence that often deliberately focuses on the spectacular. So the relevant distinction between the spectacular and the non-spectacular does not bear careful scrutiny. We have both spectacular and non-spectacular examples of the relevant data.

What we need here is a more nuanced account of the relation between the spectacular and the ordinary in all of the phenomena we have examined. Basil Mitchell has expressed the point at issue with exemplary felicity with respect to the relation between sanctity and grace. Noting that we need a more broadly theological approach that teaches us that we cannot presume to limit the divine activity to those instances in which it may be discernible to us, he continues:

> Such instances (remarkable and striking manifestations of sanctity) may be clearly revelatory . . . yet they are revelatory of the God, whose activity we believe on general grounds, to underlie even the most tentative and inarticulate movements of the human soul towards conformity with the pattern of Christ. They are like the phosphorescent crest of a wave which enables us to detect a sea whose boundaries we could not chart. Having made an entry for the concept of grace by tracing it as it breaks through more or less spectacularly into human experience, we are led to extend its application to all good works, whether characterized by the numinous or not, whether or not associated with religious belief or not. It is enough that they tend in the direction of that complete holiness, which is the "fruit of the spirit."[21]

We can surely broaden this observation. Whenever we encounter the spectacular power of God in conversion and charismatic phenomena we see but the phosphorescent crest of a wave that enables us to detect a sea of divine action and activity whose boundaries we cannot chart. We are led through these special acts of God to extend our sense of divine action in creation and providence, whether characterized by the spectacular or not. Hence they lead us into that wider vision of God that Wesley insisted was central to the whole theistic vision of the world and ourselves.

Even with this qualification, there may still be reservations about my overall revision of Wesley's vision and about my claim that we should not shy away from appeal to the argument from divine power as represented by charismatic phenomena. Clearly we may well invite ridicule and dismissal in intellectual circles when we proceed boldly down this path. Even in Christian circles mention of charismatic phenomena can set a lot of listeners' teeth on edge. In the middle of the last century in my adopted city of Dallas the two major seminaries (one generally identified as "conservative" and one as "liberal") were agreed in rejecting the existence of charismatic phenomena. Excellent scholars were fired or refused employment in both institutions because they had experienced charismatic phenomena or because they took them seriously in the history of the church. Interestingly and ironically, both institutions rejected them on epistemological grounds. The conservative seminary rejected them on the grounds that such phenomena were no longer needed once the Scriptures were canonized. Charismatic phenomena provided evidence for divine revelation in Jesus and the apostles, but now that we have an inerrant record of the divine revelation and special divine revelation has ceased, claims about such phenomena must be dismissed as demonic or as misrepresentations of natural phenomena. The liberal seminary rejected charismatic phenomena on the grounds that there was no good evidence for such phenomena, and more precisely, on the grounds that there could not be good historical evidence for such phenomena because they violated the intellectual requirements of historical criticism.[22]

What might Wesley say at this juncture? Against the first he made it clear that charismatic phenomena were not intended merely for a short time in history. He explicitly agreed with John Chrysostom that the reason for the absence of charismatic phenomena in the history of the church was "for want of faith, and virtue, and piety in those times."[23] In addition he mused over whether God had allowed the evidence of charismatic phenomena to be clogged and encumbered so that another kind of evidence might get attention. Against the second, Wesley made it clear that he did not find the epistemological arguments on offer in his day at all convincing. While he lived before the full onslaught of certain kinds of historical criticism, he clearly had deep intuitions that were at odds with the assumptions that became embedded in much historical investigation and that are already visible in the work of Conyers Middleton. Therefore we can be confident that Wesley would be equally opposed to both the conservative and liberal opposition to charismatic phenomena.

There is a deeper point, however, to be made. Wesley insisted that when it comes to matters touching our relation to God, we are never disinterested spectators merely weighing evidence. We are dealing with phenomena that call for moral and spiritual transformation. Human beings are complex truth-detecting organisms who are subject to cognitive malfunction because of the noetic effects of sin. Hence the presence of good evidence in itself will not bring us to truth or to faith. Human agents have all sorts of ways of ignoring, denying, belittling, and ridiculing evidence that is genuine. We invent both vulgar and sophisticated constructions to keep the truth at bay. We can see this manifest in individual lives; and we can see it manifest in social, academic, and political life. Recent work that flies under the banners of postmodernism and of feminist epistemology has alerted us to the way in which such factors as gender, social location, and power relations can blind us to the truth about who we are and what is really the case. Intellectuals as diverse as Michel Foucault, Edward Said, and Lorraine Code have high-lighted the way entrenched claims to impartiality, objectivity, neutrality, and the like, have served as ideological cover for commitments that are far removed from reality.

The relevance of these remarks is this: opposition to charismatic phenomena is not a neutral, objective affair. Charismatic phenomena are more than spiritual curiosity items; they signal the active presence of God in a way that invites repentance and faith. Thus opposition is to be expected. Moreover, we can anticipate that this opposition will be expressed in public and academic institutions. Cognitive malfunction is not just an individual or personal phenomenon; it is also a social and institutional phenomenon. Intellectual vice is not just personal; it is also social in nature. Much opposition to charismatic phenomenon is a matter of cognitive malfunction in the normative conventions, gate-keeping mechanisms, ethos, and practices of scholarship. Thus we must be on guard and on the lookout for deep structural problems in the grammar and technology of scholarship in this domain.

Given that intellectual opposition is well nigh inescapable, and that it is likely to mask its intellectual vice under the guise of intellectual virtue, the last thing we should do is run away and hide. To be sure, we need to be wise as serpents and innocent as doves. To be sure, it is important not to cast our pearls before swine. We need to expect to have to bear our crosses and suffer the contradiction of opponents. To be sure, we know that many will not believe should even someone rise from the dead. However, today is not a time for reserve and retreat but for advance and renewal. This is not a time for faint hearts and minds but for rigorous, intellectual boldness. This is not a time for fear but for faith. We best serve the academy not by hiding the light and power of God under a bushel but by giving a reason for the hope that is within us. We best serve our cultures not by cutting back on the evidence but by patiently making all the evidence at our disposable available. We best serve the gospel not by shying away from the promises of God but by the fulfillment of those promises (all the promises) in our midst today. Included is the promise of the power of God, a God who can do more abundantly than ever we ask or think.

Chapter 4

Faith and Divine Revelation

John Wesley was a robust rationalist in the popular sense that he readily took it upon himself to explain and give evidence of what he believed. His mother is reported to have said that he would not go to the toilet without a reason. In the technical sense he was not at all a rationalist for, with Aristotle and Locke, he held that all knowledge comes through the senses. Technically he was an empiricist, but he was a very peculiar empiricist, for he believed that there was very good experiential evidence for the reality of God.[1] Locke, Berkeley, and Hume, that great trinity of empiricism, had no place in their epistemology for this kind of evidence. For them the senses were physical senses geared toward the natural world, even though by the time of Hume the natural world, causation, and the self had evaporated from sight altogether. Moreover, Wesley's commitment to reason was not an abstract, philosophical stance; it was central in his journey of faith and to the way he conducted his ministry as a preacher of the gospel. Thus we have seen that even in his account of his Aldersgate experience he was spinning his story in a way that exhibits his appeal to a little minefield of interesting evidence. His testimony was laced with argument and tacit evidence.

His testimony was also artfully shot through with scriptural texts displayed without a hint of artificiality. This appeal to Scripture was not a bolt from the blue; nor was it merely the expression of conventional piety. In constantly referring to Scripture Wesley was integrating his claims about evidence into a larger intellectual horizon where special divine revelation played a pivotal role. In other words, Wesley combined his commitment to reason with an even stronger commitment to special divine revelation. How is this to be done with integrity? In drawing on divine revelation, was Wesley simply adding in one more piece of evidence, piling up the data line upon line in a cumulative case, in order to persuade himself and others that his case was foolproof?[2] Or does his appeal to divine revelation have to be handled in a more subtle way, so that we take note of its unusual yet privileged position in his epistemology of theology?

We first need, however, to pause and get a hold of Wesley's vision of special revelation before we can sort through this matter. When we explore Wesley's vision, we quickly discover that we have several issues on our hands. First, what basic claims does Wesley advance about special revelation? Second, how does he advance such claims? Having examined these issues we can then explore how the evidence developed heretofore is to be related to special revelation.

What basic claims does Wesley advance about special revelation? Wesley's basic claims reflect the common, orthodox theological wisdom of the day; his theory of special revelation was enshrined in his doctrine of Scripture; and his theory of Scripture was presented as a theory of divine inspiration. Special revelation is constituted by Scripture, which originates causally from God by means of divine inspiration. This vision of special revelation explains Wesley's choice of sermons as his favored genre in theology. Sermons are not lectures; they are intended to transmit the good news of salvation and to bring people into a deeper relationship with God. His choice of that genre also gave a clear signal as to the primary purpose of divine revelation: it is to enable us to find our way to heaven.

His preface to the *Sermons on Several Occasions* makes both these points with exemplary flair and clarity.

> I have thought, I am a creature of a day, passing through life as an arrow through the air. I am a spirit come from God, and returning to God: Just hovering over the great gulf; till, a few moments hence, I am no more seen; I drop into an unchangeable eternity! I want to know one thing,—the way to heaven; how to land safe on that happy shore. God himself has condescended to teach the way: For this very end he came from heaven. He hath written it down in a book. O give me that book! At any price, give me the book of God! I have it: Here is knowledge enough for me. Let me be *homo unius libri.* Here then I am, far from the busy ways of men. I sit down alone: Only God is here. In his presence I open, I read his book, for this end, to find the way to heaven. Is there a doubt concerning the meaning of what I read? Does anything appear dark or intricate? I lift up my heart to the Father of Lights: —Lord, is it not thy word, If any man lack wisdom, let him ask of God? Thou givest liberally, and upbraidest not. Thou hast said, If any be willing to do thy will, he shall know. I am willing to do, let me know, thy will. I then search after and consider parallel passages of Scripture, "comparing spiritual things with spiritual." I meditate thereon with all the attention and earnestness of which my mind is capable. If any doubt still remains, I consult those who are experienced in the things of God; and then the writings whereby, being dead, they yet speak. And what I thus learn, that I teach.[3]

Wesley's vision of Scripture was located within his wider vision of creation, freedom, the fall, and redemption. Within the process of redemption God has provided sufficient knowledge of the way to heaven in "the book of God," the "Word of God," a book whose meaning can be discerned with the aid of such practices as prayer, study, and consultation with those who are experienced in the things of God. The latter practice dovetails nicely with his more general insistence that we can actually come to experience the things of God for ourselves. It is only fitting that those looking for God should seek help from those who already know God. Yet it is clear that such experience operates hermeneutically rather than epistemologically. While we may lean on others for help in interpreting what God has said to us in Scripture, the grounds for our theological claims are not their experience at this point but the texts of Scripture. If we claim to see more clearly the truth about God, then Wesley's challenge was simple: "Point me to a better way than I have known. Show me it is so, by plain proof of Scripture."[4]

Should we say then that Wesley is a fundamentalist? Fundamentalist is not a felicitous term to apply to Wesley. It is certainly the case that Wesley can write at times like a Christian fundamentalist. Like Eve in the "Garden of Eve," he improves, for example, on the language of the Bishop of Gloucester in the latter's comments on the effects of the inspiration of Scripture. The bishop claimed that the Holy Spirit "so directed the writers, that no considerable error should fall from them."[5] Wesley added: "Nay, will not the allowing there is *any error* in Scripture, shake the authority of the whole?"[6] However, Wesley's overall vision was lodged in an Anglican vision of the Christian faith that is foreign to fundamentalism. As we have seen, Wesley was ready to give a place to evidence outside of Scripture in arguing for the truth of Christian doctrine. More importantly, he adapted the Anglican Articles for his people in North America; he gave a privileged position to the Ante-Nicene Fathers in his understanding of the Scriptures; and he readily accepted the Apostles' Creed as a summary of Scripture.

> The foundation of true religion stands upon the oracles of God. It is built upon the prophets and apostles, Jesus Christ himself being the chief corner-stone. Now of what excellent use is reason if we would either understand ourselves, or explain to others, those living oracles! And how is it possible without it to understand the essential truths contained therein? A beautiful summary of which we have in that which is called the Apostles Creed.[7]

These varied claims put Wesley in a different world from that of fundamentalism.

Interestingly, precisely the kind of evidence we have already explored showed up in his response to the second question we posed, namely, how did Wesley advance his claims for the existence of special divine revelation in Scripture?

> There are four grand and powerful arguments which strongly induce us to believe that the Bible must be from God; viz., miracles, prophecies, the goodness of the doctrine, and the moral character of the penmen. All the miracles flow from divine power; all the prophecies, from divine understanding; the goodness of the doctrine, from divine goodness; and the moral character of the penmen, from divine holiness. Thus Christianity is built upon four grand pillars; viz., the power, understanding, goodness, and holiness of God. Divine power is the source of all the miracles; divine understanding, of all the prophecies; divine goodness, of the goodness of the doctrine; and divine holiness, of the moral character of the penmen.[8]

The argument here is elliptical. Wesley has isolated four features of the content of Scripture and sought to explain the presence of these or the events to which they testify as best explicable in terms of the character and action of God. So the miracles, prophecies, the goodness of the doctrine, and the moral character of the writers are to be explained by positing a divine agent who brings them about for certain intentions and purposes. The argument presupposes that the Scriptures are historically reliable, for otherwise Wesley cannot appeal to miracles and prophecies. One cannot argue from the reliability of the Scriptures to the reliability of miracles and prophecies; the argument must proceed from the latter to the former. This reliance explains why Wesley was so astute in recognizing the threat from Conyers Middleton's arguments. Middleton was undercutting the appeal to miracle and prophecy in a very deep way, thus depriving Wesley of the historical element in his argument. The other two phenomena (the goodness of the doctrine and the moral character of the writers) clearly presuppose that we can already recognize the goodness of the doctrine and the moral character of the writers. Hence Wesley has appealed to phenomena that are not initially secured by the text of Scripture. We have to be able to see for ourselves the phenomena in question. Once they were in place, Wesley set out to find a cause for these phenomena and found it in the activity and character of God. Hence the argument is fundamentally causal in character. In this we see once again Wesley's fondness for arguments to the best explanation.

Wesley's argument to secure the divine inspiration of Scripture is a very weak argument. This quick and easy way to establish the divine origin of Scripture tells us more about Wesley's reliance on the tacit convictions of his day that it does about the strength of this argument. There are two obvious problems in it. The phenomena (miracles, prophecies, and the like) are very vague and unspecified;

we need far more details before we can get the argument off the ground. Furthermore, Wesley's presumption that we can recognize the goodness of the doctrine and the moral characters of the writers does not fit with his grim view of cognitive malfunction in human agents. In Wesley's view, sin clearly prevents us from seeing the phenomena to which he appealed with such alacrity.

Problems also arise when we look at Wesley's efforts to establish the very same conclusion from another direction. Consider the logic of the following set of moves:

> I beg leave to propose a short, clear, and strong argument to prove the divine inspiration of the holy Scriptures. The Bible must be the invention either of good men or angels, bad men or devils, or of God.
>
> 1. It could not be the invention of good men or angels; for they neither would nor could make a book, and tell lies all the time they were writing it, saying, "Thus saith the Lord," when it was their own invention.
> 2. It could not be the invention of bad men or devils; for they would not make a book which commands all duty, forbids all sin, and condemns their souls to hell to all eternity.
> 3. Therefore, I draw this conclusion that the Bible must be given by divine inspiration.[9]

The argument presented here is causal; it seeks to establish the divine origin of Scripture. The phenomena in Scripture in this instance are the claim to speak for God, the command to fulfill our duties, the forbidding of sin, and the doctrine of an eternal hell. Wesley then invites us to consider five possible causal hypotheses, each of which would explain the origination of Scripture: good men, good angels, bad men, bad angels, and God. A quick process of elimination leaves us with only one serious possibility, divine origination by way of inspiration. The problems in this are obvious. The argument is much too vague. The data are recited without any careful specification. And the leap to the conclusion is far too quick and easy. There are other alternatives not on the table that fit better with what we actually know about the origination of Scripture. In short, this drag-him-out, knock-him-down, kill-him-dead kind of argument really shows how deeply Wesley was committed to a conventional vision of Scripture as the oracles of God. It is more a reiteration and reinforcement of traditional belief than it is a really serious argument in its favor. It reminds one of Irenaeus' argument that there must be four gospels because there are four winds; the argument is carried by the claim it supports rather than vice versa.

Wesley's view that Scripture is first and foremost the oracles of God has critical ramifications for the way he handled the kind of arguments that show up in the evidence from promise fulfillment, divine perception, and the power of God. This takes us to our third query. How do these kinds of arguments relate to the appeal to special revelation?

Special divine revelation was so crucial to Wesley that he was not satisfied if he could not in the end trace everything back to this foundation. This comes out most clearly in the way that he sought to provide exegetical evidence for his epistemological proposals. He appealed to the text of Scripture itself for his claims about perception of the divine as an appropriate form of evidence for divine reality. As we saw earlier, he returned again and again to Hebrews 11:1 and Romans 8:15-16 as the crucial proof texts for his position.

It is very important to take the full measure of what is happening at this point. One way to see this is to note that Wesley has moved from a soteriological conception of Scripture as a means of grace to Scripture as a criterion for success within epistemology. Wesley has cut very deep foundations at this point. It is not just that Scripture, as the oracles of God, gives us the truth, say, about the history of Israel, or about Jesus, the afterlife, or justification by faith. It is that Scripture gives us an account of what counts as evidence for historical and theological claims. God has told us not just what is the truth at the level of history or theology but what is the truth about the proper criteria for our claims regarding history and theology. This kind of move involves a radical epistemizing of Scripture; Scripture operates not just as a norm of truth in theology and history but also as a norm for these norms. It is hard to imagine a more epistemic conception of Scripture.

This may appear terribly abstract, so let me pause and explain what is the issue here. When we worry about the truth or falsehood of our beliefs it is easy to see a varied network of questions developing. For example, someone insists that there is an intermediate state between this life and the time of the resurrection from the dead; someone else contests this by insisting that when we die, it is all over for us until we are resurrected from the dead. These claims are incompatible; they cannot both be true at the same time. So we cast around for relevant evidence. We examine different pieces of evidence, say, from near-death experiences, or from neuroscience, or from what we take to be special revelation from God. However, there are yet other kinds of questions that readily arise: What kind of evidence should we consult at this point? Why should we take special revelation to be relevant evidence? Why think that neuroscience matters? These are epistemological queries. They go below the surface and take us to another order of inquiry. We want to know what sort of evidence to seek out and apply. We can then, of course, start pressing the issue to another level and reiterate the problem. How do we resolve the problem of what counts as evidence in the debate about evidence? By this stage we

are in a state of intellectual vertigo; we have begun to sus-
pect that we are losing our minds rather than ordering them
aright.

Wesley moved to this level of analysis in his vision of
Scripture. Scripture, as the oracles of God, was the norm
of truth in answer to these questions, that is, questions as to
what counted as evidence in epistemology. Scripture was an
epistemic norm, not just a theological norm. This is what I
mean when I say that his position involved a radical epistemizing of Scripture; Scripture itself was put to work in the
field of epistemology. Clearly this is a very inflationary view
of Scripture compared to a vision that sees Scripture as a
means of grace that makes us wise unto salvation. In the latter analysis Scripture enables us to find our way to heaven;
in the former analysis Scripture is to be used not just for
this spiritual purpose but also to settle once and for all questions in epistemology. We can now take Scripture into the
philosophy seminar and quote it to resolve epistemological
questions, having in hand the highest kind of evidence available, namely, God's own proposals on epistemology.[10]

Clearly something here has gone seriously astray. In epistemology we cannot resolve disputes by appealing to divine
revelation for at least four reasons. First, the appeal to divine
revelation is itself in dispute as an epistemological category.
It is not immediately clear formally why revelation should
be taken seriously in epistemology, a fact that is revealed in
its fall from favor even within philosophy of religion over
the last half-century.[11] Revelation simply does not show up
in the field as a whole; and if it does it is treated with dis-
dain. Revelation is seen as a copout, a skyhook that cannot
connect us to a source or norm of truth. Second, if divine
revelation is a genuine category in epistemology, we cannot
secure its place by appealing to divine revelation without
begging the epistemological issue under review. Appealing to divine revelation would simply be a case of using the

results of divine revelation to establish the epistemic significance of divine revelation. Third, there are many material
claims to divine revelation available, so any appeal to divine
revelation is already a matter of dispute. We need some way
of adjudicating claims to divine revelation before we can get
it to do any heavy lifting in epistemology. Fourth, even with
revelation in hand we then need to sort through the problem
of the proper interpretation of divine revelation. Before we
know it, we are in a world where experts fly under the ban-
ner of hermeneutics.[12] Hence there is something profoundly
mistaken in the turn Wesley took when he thought he could
make revelation a foundational category that would act as
the source and foundation of all other epistemological claims
in theology.

Yet we must proceed carefully in unraveling what is at
stake. Wesley's epistemizing of Scripture is so deeply embedded in the history of Christianity that we need to explore
why this is the case and why so many ordinary Christians
and theologians are often disturbed if not terrified when it
is challenged. I am convinced that there are important spiritual, intellectual, and pastoral considerations that lurk in
the neighborhood. Moreover, I shall argue that Wesley himself shows signs of grasping a pivotal feature of the appeal to
divine revelation that is easily missed in the discussion.

One way into these issues is to note that Wesley, with
the whole of Western Christianity, was very concerned to
secure the highest form of certainty in theology. Even the
assurance that Wesley sought and found in the inner witness of the Holy Spirit was not sufficiently secure for him.
He wanted assurance that his personal assurance could be
grounded in the text of Scripture, the oracles of God. In turn
he wanted assurance that Scripture was indeed the oracles
of God, that it was given by divine inspiration. Furthermore,
Wesley was smitten in a significant way by epistemological
anxiety such that if there was the possibility of any error in

Scripture then the whole appeal to Scripture would collapse and he would be left twisting in the winds of skepticism. This is a common worry for hordes of Christians.

We can also say that Wesley wanted his whole life, including the life of the mind, to be committed to God. Thus he took seriously Paul's admonition to "bring every thought into captivity to Jesus Christ."[13] Hence his doctrine of sanctification carried cognitive overtones. These overtones were in turn intertwined with his vision of creation and salvation. The doctrine of creation led him to see his mind as a gift of God that should be used in the way God intended; and the doctrine of sin led him to expect cognitive malfunction that could only be corrected by grace and divine revelation. Given all these considerations it would be odd in the extreme if Wesley did not reach for a doctrine of revelation that would govern all his thinking, including his epistemological thinking.

Once we head down this road we have a possible explanation as to why Wesley was so uneasy with natural theology. Perhaps he had come to believe, if only incipiently and halfheartedly, that revelation and natural theology were not really compatible with each other. Maybe he was exploring the claim that only God can bear witness to God, a possibility that fits nicely with his particular love for the appeal to the inner witness of the Holy Spirit as the foundation for assurance about God. In the inner witness it is God who gives proof of God. If this is a plausible line of inquiry, then we can easily see why modern Wesleyans have readily made the transition to a Barthian vision of theology in which any attempt to look for support for divine revelation is seen as dangerous and incoherent.[14] It is dangerous because it introduces foreign elements into the heart of the Christian faith; and it is incoherent because it rejects its own best insight that only divine revelation can be the proper foundation of theology.

This extremely interesting development in the Wesleyan household does not strike me as the best way forward in preserving the tradition as a whole or even Wesley's central epistemological insights. Let me proceed by examining an important argument that seeks to secure the claim that divine revelation and the kind of arguments represented by natural theology and by Wesley's earlier appeal to non-revelatory evidence are incompatible with each other. The core of the argument is that any appeal to material outside of divine revelation represents a move to give reason or evidence a status higher than divine revelation. Thus it is both wrong in itself and it is a form of cognitive idolatry that dislodges God as the one and only one worthy of supreme allegiance. To appeal to anything outside of divine revelation is, in effect, to make whatever we appeal to more basic, foundational, and therefore more important than God. God's own self-revelation is sufficient in and of itself to secure claims about God.

There is a decisive objection to these proposals, which happily can be easily stated and appreciated. To make these claims is to confuse epistemology with ontology; it is to misread the relative and proper placing of evidence and of God in our lives. Consider this analogy: I have a daughter who (to put it mildly) is extremely important to me. Suppose I meet some folk who are skeptical about her existence; they do not believe she is real. I then proceed to persuade them by way of various arguments and evidence that she is indeed real, that she does exist. So I make use of testimony, display letters she has written, invite them to try and get in touch with her, produce her birth certificate, and so on. If someone then claimed that because I did this I was giving my daughter a status lower than the evidence I cited or explored, the mistake would be clear on its face. My daughter matters more to me than any piece of evidence I can produce.[15] It is likewise with God. With Wesley we can look for, discover, and deploy evidence for the reality of God without diminishing the ontological status of God by one whit. Taking this evidence seriously is not a matter of idolatry; it is simply pursuing the relevant intellectual issue at hand. Arguments and evidence have a critical role in resolving disputes and doubts; they can do so without being exalted into mini-deities that compete with God; it is a category mistake to think that they do. Wesley was right to pursue relevant evidence, and while he himself was not very impressed by natural theology, he did not at all rule out natural theology as a matter of principle.[16]

The difficulties and dangers that reside in Wesley's position lie elsewhere. First, Wesley is inconsistent as to what constitutes the foundation of theology. On some occasions he is a spiritual empiricist and makes the inner inspiration of the Holy Spirit the foundation. On other occasions he insists on Scripture as foundational. Strictly speaking, these two claims are at odds with each other.[17] Second, Wesley is inconsistent in the way he appeals to Scripture. On the one hand, he wants everything to be derived from Scripture. On the other hand, he deploys arguments that must in the nature of the case rely on evidence that is independent of Scripture. Indeed he has to do this in the case of his arguments for the divine origination of Scripture itself. Third, Wesley's exegesis of the relevant texts that serve to underwrite his epistemological appeal to Scripture involve a tendentious reading of them in order to make them fit his favored model of perceptual evidence for the reality of God.[18] Fourth, the whole appeal to Scripture has a way of upending elements in the Christian faith that Wesley himself held dear and that easily disappear from the life of Methodism in succeeding generations.[19]

If Wesley's account of divine revelation is as problematic as I suggest, the reader may wonder if there is anything worth salvaging. En route to such salvage work it is worth noting that nothing I have said undermines the possibility of a robust appeal to divine revelation in Christian theology. On the contrary, I think that divine revelation is a pivotal concept within the epistemology of theology. I share Wesley's conviction that divine revelation plays a crucial role in any healthy epistemology of theology. Indeed I want to rescue this crucial element in Wesley's theology for our own day.[20] Moreover, we should not lose sight of the pastoral issues that swirl around our topic. For some, abandoning Wesley's epistemic conception of Scripture is fraught with spiritual depression, in that they fear that they will lose everything they hold dear spiritually and theologically, if they abandon it. Hence we need to proceed sensitively. This is not the end of the matter, however. The pastoral concerns cut deeply in the opposite direction too. Many have lost their faith (including their Wesleyan faith) because the epistemic conception of Scripture undermined the wider classical faith to which Wesley was committed.[21] In time the quest for foolproof foundations turned back on itself in self-destruction, like a snake choking on its own tail or like a dog poisoning itself with its own vomit. This is not a pretty sight in the history of modern theology. The drive to derive everything from the scriptural text in fact introduces a virus that can destroy much more than it preserves, which is one reason why more modest epistemic conceptions of Scripture are now the conventional wisdom in some conservative theological circles. So how can we move forward and avoid the pitfalls that seem to confront us no matter which way we turn?

As I mentioned at the beginning of this chapter, one way forward would be to simply add special divine revelation as one more item of evidence in a complex cumulative case argument for Christian theism. Basil Mitchell makes this move. After identifying various pieces of evidence climaxing with appeal to conspicuous sanctity, he writes:

. . . the theist maintains, if there were a God who had
created a universe in which there could develop rational beings capable of responding to him and one another
with love and understanding, it is to be anticipated that
he would in some way communicate with them. The existence, then, of what purport to be such "revelations" is
something which tends to support the belief in a God who
has in these ways revealed himself; although here too the
support would be weakened if the historical and other
evidence appealed to were to be seriously impugned, or
if the concept of revelation were to run into intractable
philosophical difficulties. That there is a variety of claims
to be the revealed truth about God does not in itself show
that none of the claims can be justified. We need to ask
of each of them what sort of sense they make of human
experience and of one another. It is also relevant to ask
of each of them whether some other interpretation, more
satisfactory than is provided in its own terms, is available
to explain its occurrence, its character and its effects.[22]

This is one obvious way to proceed. Whatever its merits, it
fails to capture the deep place that divine revelation had to
play in Wesley's theology. Divine revelation cannot simply be
added in to the evidence as one more item alongside others. It has a privileged position in that it acts as criterion for
coherence for other claims and brings with it illuminating
resources that have to be unpacked for the whole gamut of
what we believe, including what we believe about ourselves
as cognitive agents. Surprisingly, Wesley turns out to be more
instructive on the topic of divine revelation than expected.

Consider the very interesting comments that Wesley
made on the place of Scripture in making decisions about
miraculous events in the history of the church. Middleton
had asserted that if we cannot believe the miracles attested
to by the later Fathers, then we ought not to believe those

that are attested to by the earliest writers of the church. Wesley insisted that Middleton had missed a crucial distinction:

> The consequence is not good; because the case is not the same with the one and with the other. Several objections, which do not hold with regard to the earlier, may lie against the later, miracles; drawn either from the improbability of the facts themselves, *such as we have no precedent of in holy writ*; from the incompetency of the instruments said to perform them, such as bones, relics, or departed saints; or from the gross credulity of a prejudiced, or the dishonesty of an interested, relater."[23]

What Wesley was claiming here is that divine revelation (holy writ, in his terms) should operate as an overrider for claims about miracles in the present. In other words, once divine revelation is in place, it has a privileged position in evaluating other claims. If claims in fact contradict special divine revelation, then that is a good reason for rejecting such claims. Thus if someone reports a miracle in which one person miraculously poisons another with water, the whole matter will be dismissed immediately as false. We will not wait to check out the veracity of the agents, the facts of the case and so on. There is already very good reason to think that something has gone wrong in the initial perception. The report in question is incompatible with standing revelation, revelation already accepted.

The same logic appeals to claims made about later divine revelation, say, in Baron Swedenborg. New claims to divine revelation have to be coherent with the vision of revelation already in hand; they have to be tested against Scripture. We can see this in Wesley's scathing assessment of Baron Swedenborg's claims to revelation.

> I sat down to read and seriously consider some of the writings of Baron Swedenborg. I began with huge prejudice

in his favour, knowing him to be a pious man, one of a strong understanding, of much learning, and one who thoroughly believed himself. But I could not hold out long. Any one of his visions puts his real character out of doubt; He is one of the most ingenious, lively, entertaining madmen that ever set pen to paper. But his waking dreams are so wild, so far remote both from Scripture and common sense, that one might as easily swallow the stories of "Tom Thumb," or "Jack the Giant-Killer."[24]

What Wesley has grasped is that divine revelation is a threshold concept. We must indeed test claims to divine revelation; otherwise we are at the mercy of charlatans or false prophets. Hence Wesley was in principle correct to press for relevant evidence in favor of any proposed revelation. Once adopted, however, revelation immediately governs all our thinking; it does so because what we now possess is divine testimony. In divine revelation we have access to nothing less than the mind of God. Given that such knowledge is the highest knowledge available, it must trump all other claims to knowledge.[25] Hence it operates as a necessary condition of the truth claims we advance; everything else we now say must cohere with what we take to be divine revelation. This is why Wesley naturally insists that the theist must reject claims to miracles that have no precedent in divine revelation or that contradict divine revelation.

We have stumbled upon the tip of a very important epistemological iceberg; much lies below the surface for further exploration. Suffice it to finish this conversation by drawing attention to a brief laundry list of claims elsewhere in Wesley that dovetail with this account of the place of divine revelation in theology. First, we can see why Wesley was intent on mining Scripture for epistemological insights. Scripture contains all sorts of epistemic suggestions and insights that are worth exploring, even though we may want to unpack the significance of the ones he favors very differently from him. Second, we can explain why Wesley began to think theologically about our intellectual capacities. Once we see ourselves in the light of divine revelation, we perceive ourselves as fallen and redeemed, and these claims have epistemic overtones. Third, in moral theology, we can begin to recognize the astute way in which Wesley began to develop a vision of divine revelation as the moral law of God that would enrich our conscience, itself seen as a gift of God, though badly damaged by sin. Thus Wesley has a deft way of recognizing the ultimate, non-negotiable appeal to Christ in the epistemology of ethics.

Above all we can see why for Wesley reflecting at a deep level on that nature of our intellectual explorations is not just an abstract philosophical investigation. The Christian life is a journey from sin to holiness. Within this journey we are to use all our cognitive capacities to the fullest. Conversion cannot in this vision be reduced to some sort of emotional, ecstatic experience. In conversion we rely on the promises of God; we hear the voice of God within through the inner witness of the Holy Spirit; we begin to perceive the truth about ourselves and about God, as it is revealed in the face of Jesus Christ; we see the power of God at work in others; and we begin to experience the power of God, however feebly, in ourselves. In the end we encounter the full splendor of God in the special revelation of His Son brought home inwardly through the secret action of the Holy Spirit. Once this occurs, we are in the New World of faith. As we live in that world, we are drawn into the love and holiness of God and sent forth to love and serve our neighbor. Equally, as we live in that world, we experience cognitive dissonance that can only be relieved by exploring the full ramifications of divine revelation for everything we know and ponder. Part of what we ponder is rationality and knowledge in and of themselves. Wesley took the revelation of God to have a bearing on such matters. We do well to engage him in that conversation. When we do so, we discover that knowledge (even knowledge about knowledge) is never far from vital piety.

> Unite the pair so long disjoined
>   Knowledge and vital piety,
> Learning and holiness combined,
>   And truth and love let all men see
> In these whom up to Thee we give,
>   Thine, wholly thine to die and live.[26]

Notes

CHAPTER 1

1   W. Reginald Ward and Richard P. Heitzenrater, eds., *The Works of John Wesley*, vol. 18 (Nashville: Abingdon, 1988), xviii, 249–50.

2   For an interesting set of essays on Wesley's Aldersgate experience, see Randy Maddox, *Aldersgate Reconsidered* (Nashville: Abingdon, 1990).

3   For a comprehensive overview of Methodism see William J. Abraham and James E. Kirby, eds., *The Oxford Handbook of Methodist Studies* (Oxford: Oxford University Press, 2009).

4   Richard P. Heitzenrater, "Great Expectations: Aldersgate and the Evidences of Genuine Christianity," in *Mirror and Memory: Reflections on Early Methodism* (Nashville: Abingdon, 1989), 106–49.

5   The classical arguments are the cosmological, teleological, and ontological arguments for the existence of God. Understood as proofs they needed to meet the exacting standards of validity (the conclusion had to follow of necessity from the premises) and soundness (the premises had to be true).

6   Albert C. Outler, ed., *The Works of John Wesley* (Nashville: Abingdon, 1985), 2:594–95.

7   "From the creation they inferred the being of a Creator, powerful and wise, just and merciful." See "Walking by Faith and Walking by Sight," in Outler, 4:52.

8   Wesley is clearly drawn to the tradition of "*o felix culpa*" (O Happy
    Fall) in his response to the problem of evil. See "God's Love to
    Fallen Man," in Outler, 2:423–35.

9   The whole attempt to explore Wesley's epistemology in terms
    of the so-called Wesleyan Quadrilateral of Scripture, tradition,
    reason and experience is useless at this point. The epistemic
    concepts deployed in the Quadrilateral are much too generic
    and abstract; we need to pay detailed attention to the precise
    epistemic moves employed by Wesley.

10 Ward and Heitzenrater, 18:249.

11 Ward and Heitzenrater, 18:253–54. Emphasis added.

12 Ward and Heitzenrater, 18:248–49.

13 Ward and Heitzenrater, 18:249–50.

14 I agree with the formula developed by William P. Alston on the
    logic of the issue as laid out in his "The Fulfillment of Promises
    as Evidence for Religious Belief," in *Faith in Theory and Practice,
    Essays on Justifying Religious Belief*, ed. Elizabeth S. Radcliffe and
    Carol J. White (Chicago: Open Court, 1993), 1–34. See especially
    the formulation of the more general argument he deploys on
    page 7. This is a seminal essay on the whole topic of fulfillment
    of divine promises as evidence for Christian belief.

15 "A Letter to the Reverend Doctor Conyers Middleton Occasioned
    by his late 'Free Inquiry,'" in *The Works of John Wesley*, ed. Thomas
    Jackson (Grand Rapids: Baker Book House, 1979), 10:79. As Wesley
    tends to run the argument informally with other arguments and
    in a way that does not fully capture what is at stake, I have taken
    the liberty of stating the argument as cleanly as I can before
    turning to Wesley's longer formulation below.

16 "A Letter to the Reverend," in Jackson, 10:78–79. Wesley switches
    horses toward the end, moving from promise-fulfillment to per-
    ception of the divine, but we can still see the promise-fulfillment
    argument peeping through.

17 I have sought to articulate this vision in *Wesley For Armchair Theo-
    logians* (Louisville: Westminster John Knox, 2005).

18 This insight needs to be handled carefully; it is easy to drop
    the theological substance of the Christian faith in the name of
    practicality and bogus piety. Moreover, Wesley ran the deep risk
    of becoming so anthropocentric that the theocentric center of
    gravity essential to a robust faith readily collapses. For more on

this see my "The End of Wesleyan Theology" in *Wesleyan Theological Journal* 40 (2005): 7–25.

19 There are interesting biographical issues in the neighborhood about the place of Aldersgate in the long-haul views of Wesley that I cannot deal with here.

20 Wesley really needs a richer and more nuanced account of both his own spiritual pilgrimage and of the Christian life as a whole, but that is a topic for another time and place.

21 "We may yet further observe that every command in Holy Writ is only a covered promise." See Outler, 1:554–55.

22 The full story summarized here can be found in David Aikman, *Jesus in Beijing: How Christianity Is Transforming China and Changing the Global Balance of Power* (Washington, D.C.: Regnery, 2003), 271–75.

23 This is one of the critical issues pursued by Wesley in his "Sixth Letter to Mr. John Smith," in Jackson, 12:56–104.

24 For an interesting account of anecdotal evidence see Jesse Hobbes, "Religious and Scientific Uses of Anecdotal Evidence," in *Faith in Theory and Practice, Essays on Justifying Religious Belief*, ed. Elizabeth S. Radcliffe and Carol J. White (Chicago: Open Court, 1993), 8–169. Alvin Goldman's *Knowledge in a Social World* (Oxford: Clarendon, 1999) provides a fine discussion of the relation between epistemology and the social world.

25 I write circumspectly here because it is also the case that elements in Wesley's theology can readily serve to undermine the faith of the church even though he thought he was upholding primitive Christianity.

26 Ward and Heitzenrater, 18:249. See n. 10 above.

CHAPTER 2

1 "On the Discoveries of Faith," in Outler, 4:28–38, and "On Faith," in Outler, 4:188–200.

2 "The Witness of the Spirit, I," in Outler, 1:267–84, and "The Witness of the Spirit, II," in Outler, 1:285–98.

3 This claim stands secure even if we rework, as we should, Wesley's particular account of original sin.

4 See "On the Education of Children," in Outler, 3:347–60.

5 Interestingly, Wesley believes that we will have appropriate senses when we get to heaven itself. See "On Faith," in Outler, 4:192.

6 Wesley quotes the last half of this verse in "On Eternity," in Outler, 1:369.

7 Wesley, "The Witness of the Spirit, I," 282.

8 I follow one of the many summaries available. See Alvin Plantinga, *Warranted Christian Belief* (New York: Oxford University Press, 2000), 156.

9 Plantinga, 184. Chapter 7, "Sin and Its Cognitive Consequences," is a brilliant exposition of the noetic effects of sin.

10 Plantinga, 243-44. It is striking how many of the scriptural texts that Wesley deploys show up in Plantinga's analysis, especially Hebrews 11:1, Romans 8:16, and Jeremiah 17:9. Plantinga draws richly on Aquinas, Luther, and Calvin in his analysis. Clearly he is drawing on a network of themes that were present in the Christian tradition during the Medieval and Reformation periods. Plantinga quotes Wesley's Aldersgate experience but prefers a reading of it that focuses on faith as a cognitive gift and rejects an analysis that works from the idea of perception of the divine. See also Plantinga, 288.

11 Alston's book, *Perceiving God: The Epistemology of Religious Experience* (Ithaca, N.Y.: Cornell University Press, 1991), has become a classic in the field.

12 He returned to faith much later in life.

13 Alston, *Perceiving God*, 224.

14 For a very different way of unpacking the logic of Wesley's claims see Richard Swinburne, *The Existence of God* (Oxford: Clarendon, 1979), chap. 13, and Caroline Franks Davis, *The Evidential Force of Religious Experience* (Oxford: Clarendon, 1989).

15 On this score Wesley fits into a long line of Anglican thinkers from Hooker through Butler, Newman, Tennant, Basil Mitchell, and Richard Swinburne who appeal to a constellation of considerations to secure a conclusion.

16 "Witness of the Spirit, II," in Outler, 1:298.

17 Even then it was subordinate to the appeal to Scripture. The tension between appeal to experience and the appeal to Scripture creates interesting challenges for Wesley and for the Methodist tradition that I discuss in "The Epistemology of Conversion: Is There Something New?" in *Conversion in the Wesleyan Tradition*, ed. Kenneth J. Collins and John H. Tyson (Nashville: Abingdon, 2001), 175-94.

18   "Letter to Mr. Smith," in Jackson, 12:100.
19   Moser's more general work in epistemology is of the highest
      quality; he is set to become one of the leading figures in philoso-
      phy of religion in the decades ahead.
20   Paul K. Moser, "Cognitive Idolatry and Divine Hiding," in *Divine
      Hiddenness*, ed. D. Howard-Snyder and P. K. Moser (Cambridge:
      Cambridge University Press, 2002). Other essays of Moser that
      are worth consulting are: "Cognitive Inspiration and Knowledge
      of God," in *The Rationality of Theism*, ed. P. Copan and P. K. Moser
      (London: Routledge, 2003); "Cognitive Grace, Filial Knowledge,
      and Gethsemane Struggle," in *For Faith and Clarity*, ed. J. Beilby
      (Grand Rapids: Baker Academic, 2006); and *Why Isn't God More
      Obvious? Finding the God who Hides and Seeks* (RZIM Critical Ques-
      tions Series). Much of this material is available at his home web-
      site. For a full dress articulation of his proposals see *The Elusive
      God: Reorienting Religious Epistemology* (Cambridge: Cambridge Uni-
      versity Press, 2008).
21   Moser, "Cognitive Idolatry and Divine Hiding." This is readily
      available at http://www.luc.edu/faculty/pmoser/idolanon/index.
      shtml, accessed on 1 April 2009. Emphasis in original.
22   Moser, "Cognitive Idolatry."
23   Moser, "Cognitive Idolatry."
24   Moser, "Cognitive Idolatry." Emphasis in original.
25   Moser, "Cognitive Idolatry." Emphasis in original.
26   Moser, "Cognitive Idolatry."
27   Moser, "Cognitive Idolatry."
28   Wesley was such a workaholic that even on the other side we get
      to help on the side of the devil or of God. See "The Discoveries of
      Faith," in Outler, 4:33, on the options available.
29   See William J. Abraham, Jason E. Vickers, and Natalie B. Van Kirk,
      eds., *Canonical Theism: A Proposal for Theology and the Church* (Grand
      Rapids: Eerdmans, 2008).

CHAPTER 3
1   The critical site here is to be found in "A Letter to the Reverend,"
      in Jackson, 10:1–79. Wesley does not use the language of charis-
      matic phenomena, but this is clearly what he has in mind, so it is
      an apt contemporary description.
2   In a way the whole charge of "enthusiasm" against Wesley and the
      Methodists was precisely that they were lacking in commitment

to reason and were carried away by illusory divine inspiration energized by emotionalism.

3 "Upon our Lord's Sermon on the Mount, IV," in Outler, 1:531. Emphasis added.

4 1 Corinthians 15:10.

5 "Upon our Lord's Sermon on the Mount, IV," in Outler, 1:531.

6 Conspicuous sanctity is, of course, also a matter of charismatic activity, but I will simply follow a distinction commonly made in popular Christian discourse.

7 Middleton's target was Roman Catholic claims to perform miracles as a sign of true continuity in the church, but he took a sideswipe at what appear to be similar phenomena among Methodists.

8 "A Letter to the Reverend," in Jackson, 10:3.

9 "A Letter to the Reverend," in Jackson, 10:3.

10 Even then Wesley wanted to defend his favorites beyond the third century, like Macarius and Ephrem Syrus. However, he clearly wants to tackle Middleton on a specific stretch of the early history rather than ramble all over the place.

11 "A Letter to the Reverend," in Jackson, 10:40.

12 "A Letter to the Reverend," in Jackson, 10:41.

13 Wesley very carefully draws the relevant distinctions between the miracles he wants to defend in the first three centuries and those that occur in the fourth century. "From page 127 to page 158, you relate miracles said to be wrought in the fourth century. I have no concern with these; but I must weigh an argument which you intermix therewith again and again. It is in substance this: 'If we cannot believe the miracles attested by the later Fathers, then we ought not to believe those which are attested by the earliest writers of the Church.' I answer, 'The consequence is not good; *because the case is not the same with the one and with the other. Several objections, which do not hold with regard to the earlier, may lie against the later, miracles; drawn either from the improbability of the facts themselves, such as we have no precedent of in holy writ; from the incompetency of the instruments said to perform them, such as bones, relics, or departed saints; or from the gross credulity of a prejudiced, or the dishonesty of an interested, relater.'*" "Letter to the Reverend," in Jackson, 10:57; emphasis added.

14 "A Letter to the Reverend," in Jackson, 10:73.

15 "A Letter to the Reverend," in Jackson, 10:75.

16 "A Letter to the Reverend," in Jackson, 10:75.

17 "A Letter to the Reverend," in Jackson, 10:75.

18 "A Letter to the Reverend," in Jackson, 10:76–77.

19 "A Letter to the Reverend," in Jackson, 10:77.

20 And, we can be sure, sometimes in the very name of Wesley himself.

21 Basil Mitchell, "The Grace of God," in *Faith and Logic: Oxford Essays in Philosophical Theology*, ed. Basil Mitchell (London: George Allen & Unwin, 1957), 174.

22 Things have changed dramatically in the "liberal" seminary since then, so much so that some critics now worry about its liberal identity.

23 "A Letter to the Reverend," in Jackson, 10:2.

CHAPTER 4

1 In this, of course, Wesley stood within a long line of theologians reaching back to Origen and beyond who had a very robust doctrine of the spiritual senses.

2 This is essentially the way that Basil Mitchell seeks to resolve the relation between revelation and other evidence for the reality of God in his pioneering work on cumulative case arguments for Christian theism. See "The Nature of a Cumulative Case," in Basil Mitchell, *The Justification of Religious Belief* (London: Macmillan, 1973), chap. 3.

3 John Wesley, *Sermons on Several Occasions* (London: Epworth, 1944), 6.

4 Wesley, *Sermons*, 9. More generally Wesley makes it clear that Scripture is the final authority for faith. "But the Christian rule of right and wrong is the word of God, the writings of the Old and New Testament; all that the Prophets and 'holy men of old' wrote 'as they were moved by the Holy Ghost;' all that Scripture which was given by inspiration of God, and which is indeed profitable for doctrine, or teaching the whole will of God; for reproof of what is contrary thereto; for correction of error; and for instruction, or training us up, in righteousness. (2 Tim iii.16.) This is a lantern unto a Christian's feet, and a light in all his paths. This alone he receives as his rule of right or wrong, of whatever is really good or evil. He esteems nothing good, but what is here enjoined, either directly or by plain consequence; he accounts nothing evil but what is here forbidden, either in terms, or by

undeniable inference. Whatever the Scripture neither forbids nor enjoins, either directly or by plain consequence, he believes to be of an indifferent nature; to be in itself neither good nor evil; this being the whole and sole outward rule whereby his conscience is to be directed in all things." See "Witness of Our Own Spirit," in Outler, 1:302–3.

5　"Letter to the Bishop of Gloucester," in Jackson, 9:150.

6　"Letter to the Bishop of Gloucester," in Jackson, 9:150. Emphasis added. It is worth noting that Wesley allowed for "mistakes" to be taken over from the Jewish historians quoted, for example, by Matthew. See his comment on Matthew 1:1 in *Explanatory Notes upon the New Testament* (London: Epworth, 1941), 15.

7　"The Case of Reason Impartially Considered," in Outler, 2:591–92.

8　"A Clear and Concise Demonstration of the Divine Inspiration of the Holy Scriptures," in Jackson, 6:484.

9　"A Clear and Concise Demonstration," in Jackson, 6:484.

10　In his review of Locke's *An Essay Concerning Human Understanding*, Wesley criticized Locke's position on species and their essences on the grounds that Locke did not agree with Moses. Later Wesley appealed to Scripture to overturn the claim that "It is a false supposition, that there are certain precise essences by which things are distinguished into species." Wesley clearly thought that Scripture was a norm in epistemology, to the extent that any philosophical thesis had to be compatible with Scripture. It is hard to see how Scripture even begins to speak to the issues Wesley raised here. See "Remarks Upon Mr. Locke's 'Essay On Human Understanding,'" in Jackson, 13:461–62.

11　The fine works by George Mavrodes, Richard Swinburne, and Keith Ward are the exceptions that prove the rule at this point. See George Mavrodes, *Revelation in Religious Belief* (Philadelphia: Temple University Press, 1988); Richard Swinburne, *Revelation: From Metaphor to Analogy* (Oxford: Clarendon, 1992); and Keith Ward, *Religion and Revelation* (Oxford: Clarendon, 1994).

12　Wesley was well aware of the importance of getting the interpretation of revelation straight. His concern was nicely exhibited in his reply to John Smith. Smith had complained that Wesley had failed to see that the issue between him and his antagonists was "not whether such words are Scripture, but whether they are to be so interpreted." Wesley stoutly replied: "You surprise me! I take your word, else I should never have imagined you had read over the latter Appeal; so great a part of which is employed in this very thing, in fighting my way inch by inch; in proving, not such words are Scripture, but that they must be interpreted in the manner there set down." See "Letter to Mr. Smith," in Jackson, 12:63.

13 2 Corinthians 10:4. See the sermon "Wandering Thoughts," in Outler, 2:125–37.

14 Several leading Wesleyans have taken this route in the last half-century: Robert E. Chiles, John Deschner, Donald Dayton, Craig Keen, and Stanley Hauerwas. See especially Hauerwas' Gifford lectures, *With the Grain of the Universe: The Church's Witness and Natural Theology* (Grand Rapids: Brazos, 2001).

15 I leave the reader to explore a variation on this analogy that would posit the potential existence of a daughter whom I did not know that I had fathered! Suppose my wife has secretly borne a daughter of mine that she had kept hidden from me. She has had the baby secretly adopted by one of her sisters. In this case too, any evidence that would convince me of this fact would not settle at all the issue of the ontological status of this daughter in my life.

16 There is, of course, the possibility of making the life of the mind more important than God; this would be a form of idolatry, but that is a rabbit I shall refrain from chasing here.

17 I have explored this tension in "The Epistemology of Conversion."

18 I have explored the appeal to the inner witness in "The Epistemological Significance of the Inner Witness of the Holy Spirit," in *Faith and Philosophy* 7 (1990): 434–50; and I have explored Hebrews 11:1 in "Faith, Assurance, and Conviction: An Epistemological Commentary on Hebrews 11:1," in *Ex Auditu* 19 (2003): 65–75.

19 I have argued the more general claim at stake at length in my *Canon and Criterion in Christian Theology* (Oxford: Clarendon, 1998). I have suggested that this is the case in Wesleyan theology in "The End of Wesleyan Theology" in *Wesleyan Theological Journal*, 40 (2005): 7–25.

20 This is the burden of *Crossing the Threshold of Divine Revelation* (Grand Rapids: Eerdmans, 2006).

21 It would be wonderful to have a list of those who have suffered this fate, but I leave that matter to historians.

22 Mitchell, *Justification*, 42.

23 "A Letter to the Reverend," in Jackson, 10:75. Emphasis added.

24 See Ward and Heitzenrater, 22:217-18. Wesley provides a fuller account of this move in his "Thoughts on the Writings of Baron Swedenborg," in Jackson, 13:425-48. The final parting shot makes clear the privileged place Wesley gives to Scripture in assessing new claims to divine revelation. After citing a host of relevant biblical texts, he continues: "Who illuminated either Jacob Behmen, or Baron Swedenborg, flatly to contradict these things? It could not be the God of the holy Prophets; for He is always consistent with himself. Certainly it was the spirit of darkness. And indeed 'the light which was in them was darkness,' while they laboured to kill the never-dying worm, and to put out the unquenchable fire! And with what face can any that profess to believe the Bible, give any countenance to these dreamers? that filthy dreamer, in particular, who takes care to provide harlots, instead of fire and brimstone, for the devils and damned spirits in hell! O my brethren, let none of you that fear God recommend such a writer any more! much less labour to make the deadly poison palatable, by sweetening it with all care! All his folly and nonsense we may excuse; but not his making God a liar; not his contradicting, in so open and flagrant a manner, the whole oracles of God! True, his tales are often exceeding lively, and as entertaining as the tales of the fairies: But I dare not give up my Bible for them; and I must give up one or the other. If the preceding extracts are from God, then the Bible is only a fable: But if 'all Scriptures are given by inspiration of God,' then let these dreams sink into the pit from whence they came." Jackson, 13:447-48.

25 This point was well known to Thomas Aquinas and Richard Hooker but has been lost in the modern discussion. I explore its full ramifications in *Crossing the Threshold*.

26 Frank Baker, ed., *Representative Verse of Charles Wesley* (Nashville: Abingdon, 1962), 143.

Bibliography

Abraham, William J. *Canon and Criterion in Christian Theology*. Oxford: Clarendon, 1998.

———. *Crossing the Threshold of Divine Revelation*. Grand Rapids: Eerdmans, 2006.

———. "The End of Wesleyan Theology." *Wesleyan Theological Journal* 40 (2005): 7–25.

———. "The Epistemological Significance of the Inner Witness of the Holy Spirit." *Faith and Philosophy* 7 (1990): 434–50.

———. "The Epistemology of Conversion: Is There Something New?" In *Conversion in the Wesleyan Tradition*, edited by Kenneth Collins and John H. Tyson, 175–94. Nashville: Abingdon, 2001.

———. "Faith, Assurance, and Conviction: An Epistemological Commentary on Hebrews 11:1." *Ex Auditu* 19 (2003): 65–75.

———. *Wesley for Armchair Theologians*. Louisville: Westminster John Knox, 2005.

Abraham, William J., and James E. Kirby, eds. *The Oxford Handbook of Methodist Studies*. Oxford: Oxford University Press, 2009.

Abraham, William J., Jason E. Vickers, and Natalie B. Van Kirk, eds. *Canonical Theism: A Proposal for Theology and the Church*. Grand Rapids: Eerdmans, 2008.

Aikman, David. *Jesus in Beijing: How Christianity Is Transforming China and Changing the Global Balance of Power.* Washington, D.C.: Regnery, 2003.

Alston, William P. "The Fulfillment of Promises as Evidence for Religious Belief." In *Faith in Theory and Practice, Essays on Justifying Religious Belief,* edited by Elizabeth S. Radcliffe and Carol J. White, 1–34. Chicago: Open Court, 1993.

———. *Perceiving God: The Epistemology of Religious Experience.* Ithaca, N.Y.: Cornell University Press, 1991.

Baker, Frank, ed. *Representative Verse of Charles Wesley.* Nashville: Abingdon, 1962.

Davis, Caroline Franks. *The Evidential Force of Religious Experience.* Oxford: Clarendon, 1989.

Goldman, Alvin I. *Knowledge in a Social World.* Oxford: Clarendon, 1999.

Hauerwas, Stanley. *With the Grain of the Universe: The Church's Witness and Natural Theology.* Grand Rapids: Brazos, 2001.

Heitzenrater, Richard P. "Great Expectations: Aldersgate and the Evidences of Genuine Christianity." In *Mirror and Memory: Reflections on Early Methodism,* 106–49. Nashville: Abingdon, 1989.

Hobbes, Jesse. "Religious and Scientific Uses of Anecdotal Evidence." In *Faith in Theory and Practice, Essays on Justifying Religious Belief,* edited by Elizabeth S. Radcliffe and Carol J. White, 8–169. Chicago: Open Court, 1993.

Jackson, Thomas, ed. *The Works of John Wesley.* Vols. 10–13. Grand Rapids: Baker Book House, 1979.

Maddox, Randy L., ed. *Aldersgate Reconsidered.* Nashville: Abingdon, 1990.

Mavrodes, George I. *Revelation in Religious Belief.* Philadelphia: Temple University Press, 1988.

Mitchell, Basil. "The Grace of God." In *Faith and Logic: Oxford Essays in Philosophical Theology,* edited by Basil Mitchell, 149–75. London: Allen & Unwin, 1957.

———. *The Justification of Religious Belief.* London: Macmillan, 1973.

Moser, Paul K. "Cognitive Idolatry and Divine Hiding." In *Divine Hiddenness*, edited by D. Howard-Snyder and P. K. Moser, 120–48. Cambridge: Cambridge University Press, 2002.

———. "Cognitive Inspiration and Knowledge of God." In *The Rationality of Theism*, edited by P. Copan and P. K. Moser, 55–71. London: Routledge, 2003.

———. "Reorienting Religious Epistemology: Cognitive Grace, Filial Knowledge, and Gethsemane Struggle." In *For Faith and Clarity*, edited by J. Beilby, 65–81. Grand Rapids: Baker Academic, 2006.

———. *The Elusive God: Reorienting Religious Epistemology.* Cambridge: Cambridge University Press, 2008.

———. *Why Isn't God More Obvious? Finding the God Who Hides and Seeks.* RZIM Critical Questions Series, 2000. www.luc.edu/faculty/pmoser/idolanon/GodMoreObvious.pdf

———, ed. *Idolaters Anonymous.* http://www.luc.edu/faculty/pmoser/idolanon/relWrit.shtml.

Outler, Albert C. *The Works of John Wesley.* Vols. 1–4. Nashville: Abingdon, 1984–2003.

Plantinga, Alvin. *Warranted Christian Belief.* New York: Oxford University Press, 2000.

Swinburne, Richard. *The Existence of God.* Oxford: Clarendon, 1979.

———. *Revelation: From Metaphor to Analogy.* Oxford: Clarendon, 1992.

Ward, Keith. *Religion and Revelation: A Theology of Revelation in the World's Religions.* Oxford: Clarendon, 1994.

Ward, W. Reginald, and Richard P. Heitzenrater, eds. *The Works of John Wesley.* Vol. 18. Nashville: Abingdon, 1988.

Wesley, John. *Explanatory Notes upon the New Testament.* London: Epworth, 1941.

———. *Sermons on Several Occasions.* London: Epworth, 1944.

Index

Abraham, William J., 81n3,
  85n29, 89n17, 85n18, 85n19,
  85n20
agnosticism, 44
Aikman, David, 83n22
Aldersgate experience, 1–2
Alston, William P., 31–33, 54,
  82n14, 94n11, 84n13
analytic philosophy, 53
Apostles' Creed, 65
Aquinas, Thomas, 84n10, 90n25
Articles of Religion, Anglican
  65
assurance, 24

Baker, Frank, 90n26
Balcombe, Dennis, 17
Balcombe amendment, 19–20
Behmen, Jacob, 90n24
Beilby, J., 85n20
Berkeley, Bishop George, 39, 61

Böhler, Peter, 9
Butler, Bishop Joseph, 39, 84n15

Calvin, John, 84n10
catechesis, 39
certainty, 71
charismatic activity, 46, 54,
  86n6
Chiles, Robert E., 89n14
Chrysostom, John, 58
Code, Lorraine, 59
cognitive idolatry, 73
cognitive malfunction, 58–59,
  72
Collins, Kenneth J., 84n17
conspicuous sanctity, 44, 55,
  86n6
Constantine, 47
conversion, 55, 79
Copan, P., 85n20
creation, 57, 72